P9-DFH-440

Persuasive Public Relations for Libraries

Persuasive
Public Relations
for Libraries

Edited by
Kathleen Kelly Rummel
and Esther Perica

American Library Association
Chicago 1983

021.7
P467

Text design by Ray Machura
Cover design by Natalie Wargin
Text composed by Modern Typographers, Inc.
  in Linotron Aster. Display type, Perpetua,
  composed by Pearson Typographers.
Printed on 50-pound Glatfelter, a pH-neutral
  stock, and bound in 10-point Carolina cover
  stock by Malloy Lithographing, Inc.

Library of Congress Cataloging in Publication Data
Main entry under title:

Persuasive public relations for libraries.

  Bibliography: p.
  1. Public relations—Libraries—Addresses, essays,
lectures. 2. Libraries and society—Addresses, essays,
lectures. I. Rummel, Kathleen Kelly. II. Perica,
Esther.
Z716.3.P48 1983   021.7   83-15473
ISBN 0-8389-3284-3

Copyright © 1983 by the American Library
Association. All rights reserved except those
which may be granted by Sections 107 and
108 of the Copyright Revision Act of 1976.
Printed in the United States of America.

Contents

UNIVERSITY LIBRARIESiii
CARNEGIE-MELLON UNIVERSITY
PITTSBURGH, PENNSYLVANIA 15213

Contents

Editors and Contributors

EDITORS

Kathleen Kelly Rummel is a librarian and P.R. consultant who plans and presents workshops for library audiences. Her firm specializes in producing training programs, developing P.R. projects, conference planning, and the production of audiovisual and promotional materials for libraries and other clients. She is a past chair of the Public Relations Section of the Library Administration and Management Association (LAMA), American Library Association.

Esther Perica is the librarian at Elk Grove High School, Elk Grove Village, Illinois, and the library resources advisor at Roosevelt University's Northwest Campus in Arlington Heights, Illinois. She is a consultant and workshop leader in the areas of oral history and newspaper indexing, as well as a member of the LAMA Public Relations Section.

CONTRIBUTORS

Virginia Baeckler is the coauthor of *Go, Pep and Pop! 250 Tested Ideas for Lively Libraries* and the author of *PR for Pennies: Low-Cost Library Public Relations*. Currently, the author is conducting workshops on popular library themes and working on a new book, *Storytime Science*.

Peggy Barber is director of the Public Information Office of the American Library Association.

Janet R. Bean is director of the Chicago Public Library Cultural Center, which has visitors totaling 1¼ million, circulation over 600,000, and more than 800 programs and exhibits annually. She is a past president of the Chicago Library Club.

Sally Brickman is library editor/publicist at Case Western Reserve University Libraries. A former children's librarian and journalist, she is a specialist in the area of academic library public relations and is the 1983–84 chair of the LAMA Public Relations Section.

Carol Bryan is editor of the *Library Imagination Paper*, a P.R. clip-art quarterly for librarians, and is the owner of a graphic design and writing agency. She is the author of numerous articles on library public relations and the recipient of fifteen awards for library graphics and writing.

Margaret Chartrand is the public relations manager for the Metropolitan Toronto Library Board. Her eighteen years of experience in public relations have been spent mainly in working for public service institutions. She has also worked as a journalist for various Canadian print media.

Phil Douglis is a photographics consultant, critic, and director of the Douglis Visual Workshops.

Ann Heidbreder Eastman served as chair of the Public Relations Section of LAMA, 1982–83. She is also a member of the Executive Committee of the Center for the Book in the Library of Congress and served as coordinator of the "Books Make a Difference" project. Since 1978, she has been director of public affairs programs for the College of Arts and Sciences at Virginia Polytechnic Institute and State University.

Jon Eldredge is library director at Eastern New Mexico University–Clovis. Formerly, he was chief of outreach programs at the University of New Mexico Medical Center Library. From 1979 to 1981 he served as assistant librarian for Lake Forest College.

Before entering the field of librarianship he was program director for WBCR-FM and music director of KTDB-FM.

Joan Erwin has been the community relations coordinator for the Orlando Public Library System since 1973. Before joining libraries, she did public relations for public television stations in Kentucky and Florida. In 1980–81, she served as chair of the Public Relations Section of LAMA.

Joanne R. Euster, library director at San Francisco State University, was previously university librarian at Loyola University in New Orleans. She participated in the consultant trainee program at the Office of Management Studies of Association of Research Libraries, and is the author of *Changing Patterns in Internal Communication in Large Academic Libraries* (Office of Management Studies, 1981).

Sue Fontaine is associate chief of public relations for the New York Public Library. She is a past chair of the Public Relations Section of LAMA. A former radio and television producer, she has developed a number of courses and learning tools in the field of library P.R.

Theresa M. Fredericka is school media consultant, Ohio Department of Education. She is active in state and national library associations, especially American Association of School Librarians (AASL) and LAMA's Public Relations Section, serving on the Public Relations Services to Libraries and John Cotton Dana committees.

Mona Garvey is an artist, librarian, and P.R. consultant. She is author and illustrator of *Library Displays, Teaching Displays,* and *Library Public Relations* and designer of "Display Pack 6." She has presented public relations programs throughout the United States and Europe and her company, M.G. Associates, markets display materials.

John D. Hales, Jr., is director of the Suwannee River Regional Library, Live Oak, Florida.

Maria Hayley is the coordinator of young adult services for the

Chicago Public Library/Chicago Library System. She is active in ALA's Young Adult Services Division, including the Public Relations Committee, and was the chairperson of the YASD local arrangements for the Centennial Conference.

Dawn Heller is media services coordinator of the Riverside-Brookfield High School, Riverside, Illinois. She has served as president of both the Illinois Association for Media in Education and the Illinois Library Association. A frequent speaker and workshop leader, she is the copublisher of *Library Insights, Promotion, and Programs* (LIPP).

Pat Hogan, director of the Itasca, Illinois, Public Library, was formerly information librarian/computer coordinator, North Suburban Library System, Wheeling, Illinois. Currently she is vice-president of the Public Library Section of the Illinois Library Association, chair of the Metropolitan Chicago Library Assembly and an ALA councilor-at-large.

Peggy Howe is the information officer for the North Carolina Department of Cultural Resources, with public relations responsibilities for the State Library and Archives and History divisions. She has worked as a newspaper editor, reporter, and feature writer and as a public relations officer with United States Steel and with state government. She is the winner of several P.R. awards, including the John Cotton Dana.

Louise Condak Liebold is in charge of public relations and adult programming for the East Meadow Public Library on Long Island. She is a former newspaper reporter, radio writer/commentator, fashion publicist, and P.R. director for a large amusement park. She has served as chair of the John Cotton Dana Committee and was the originator and coordinator of the first ALA "Swap 'n' Shop."

Anne J. Mathews is an associate professor at the Graduate School of Librarianship and Information Management, University of Denver. She is a council member of the American Library Association and a member of the National Council on Quality Continuing Education, and of the board of directors of Friends of Libraries, U.S.A. She is also a consultant and workshop leader in the areas of communication, time management, public relations, and marketing.

Alice Norton operates Alice Norton Public Relations, Ridgefield, Connecticut, which provides services throughout the country to libraries and library associations. She conducts seminars and workshops on library public relations. She is a professional librarian and an accredited member of the Public Relations Society of America.

Diana Proeschel is a foreign service officer with the International Communication Agency and the director of "Amerika Haus," an information and cultural center in Stuttgart, Germany. Previously a U.S. Army Field Services librarian in Washington, D.C., she has held library positions in Thailand, Italy, Japan, France, and Germany. She is a frequent speaker on library public relations and has written a regular P.R. column for *Public Libraries*.

Florence Frette Stiles is currently president of Creative Connections in Carmel-by-the-Sea, California. She is former P.R. consultant for the State Library of Iowa and the editor of the *Iowa Trustees Library Guide*. She has served on many ALA public relations committees, including chair of the ALA National Library Week Committee and chair of the Public Relations Section of LAMA. She is accredited by the Public Relations Society of America.

Ann Montgomery Tuggle is media coordinator of the West Chicago Elementary District and coeditor and publisher of *Library Insights, Promotions, and Programs*.

Preface

This book presents a potpourri of articles about effective library public relations. Geared to readers interested in better promotion for all types of libraries, it includes a myriad of materials and ideas contributed by leading public relations (P.R.) practitioners from around the nation. It is not a comprehensive manual; many marketing and publicity topics were necessarily omitted and are waiting in the wings for inclusion in the next Library Administration and Management Association (LAMA) Public Relations Section publication effort. It is, however, a very useful handbook for those interested in considering and improving their library's public relations program.

Part One, Aims of Public Relations, highlights thoughtful insights on the future of library public relations, as well as on the meaning of marketing for libraries and on the importance of planning.

Part Two, Some Special Audiences, pays special attention to public relations approaches in public libraries, school media programs, college and university libraries, and library systems. A P.R. review of a selection of library roles and audiences is also included.

Part Three, Skills for Public Relations, is brimming full of "how-to-do-it" tips, including practical advice on producing and using graphics, photography, news releases, public service announcements, and annual reports.

Part Four, Some Special Resources, offers information about ALA public relations support services, including National Library Week activities and the John Cotton Dana Awards program. A step-by-step guide to planning a P.R. workshop and a helpful bibliography complete the section.

This book is the second in a series of publications sponsored by the Public Relations Section of the Library Administration and Management Association, a division of ALA. The first in the series, *PRepare: The Library Public Relations Recipe Book*, was published in 1978 and is an excellent resource still available from the LAMA office, 50 East Huron Street, Chicago, Illinois 60611. We recommend it. This publication, PERSUASIVE PUBLIC RELATIONS FOR LIBRARIES, furthers the Public Relations Section's goal of developing and supporting library P.R. literature. More publications on this topic are planned.

We would like to thank Roger Parent, Executive Director of the Library Administration and Management Association, and the former chairpersons of the Public Relations Section—Joan Erwin, Florence Stiles, and Ann Eastman—for support and cooperation on this project. We also wish to acknowledge Theana Vavasis, Roosevelt University, Rolling Meadows High School, Sugarplum Enterprises, and the staff of K.R. Communications for their editorial and production assistance.

Almost all the information in this book can be applied to improving public relations for *any* type of library. We believe the principles of effective marketing, public relations, and publicity are equally meaningful to public, school, academic, and special libraries. The challenge to all librarians is to creatively interpret these principles to fit individual library needs and goals and to acquire the communication skills that can catapult any library into the competition for the public's interest and support.

KATHLEEN KELLY RUMMEL
ESTHER PERICA

Part One

Aims of
Public Relations

Anne J. Mathews

Public Relations in Context: Marketing the Library

While marketing encompasses the whole process of exchanging goods and services, public relations (P.R.) involves the communication and promotional aspects of that exchange. In the following overview of marketing, there is a discussion of the role of P.R. within the general context of marketing library services.

Marketing is directed at satisfying needs and wants, or offering a perceivable benefit to the consumer, through an exchange process. Exchange is the central concept underlying marketing.[1] It is necessary, in marketing, to understand people's needs, to design offerings to satisfy those needs, and to inform people effectively of the value of using the offering to satisfy their needs. In some instances, it may be necessary to actually create a desire or need for a product or service.

The concept of exchange applies to libraries in that they offer materials or services in exchange for monies and other kinds of support. In public and school libraries, the money comes from taxes, in private colleges and universities from fees, and in special libraries from research funds. Although the money is more or less guaranteed in some of these cases, a marketing orientation is appropriate for libraries, because the kind and quality of service a library offers affects the amount of support, financial or other, that it receives.

ORGANIZATIONAL OBJECTIVES AND MARKETING

Marketing aims "to bring about voluntary exchanges of value with target markets for the purpose of achieving organizational

Portions of this article appear in Anne J. Mathews, "The Use of Marketing Principles in Library Planning," in Darlene E. Weingard, ed., *Marketing for Libraries and Information Agencies* (Norwood, N.J.: Ablex Publishing, 1983).

objectives."[2] If the purpose of marketing is to achieve an organization's objective, it is essential that the organization clearly define its purpose and the objectives of its program. Effective marketing planning requires being very specific about the target objectives: in the commercial sector the major objective is, most often, profit. In the noncommercial or nonprofit sector, the major objective is usually public interest or service. A library must establish its goals on the basis of input from trustees, faculty, the public, administration, etc. What is the purpose of your library? What are your goals? Does anyone know?

Having identified your goals, it is then important that your objectives be developed in order that those goals can be achieved. Objectives, as we all know, must be specific, measurable, and have a time frame. For example, a public library designs a registration campaign with the objective of registering 300 new users by September 1st of the coming year. This may be further refined to designate a particular area of the city or a specific target group—perhaps the elderly or the primary-grade school children or young adults. In another instance a university library plans a series of one-hour demonstrations of computer-based searching techniques to introduce faculty to data bases in their disciplines. From October 1 through November 15, each Monday from 3:00 to 4:00 P.M., various departments (target markets) will be invited to come to the library. In each of these examples, an objective is established and a specific *program* is designed to carry out the purpose of the objective.

MARKET SEGMENTATION

Market segmentation is a tool that aims at ensuring that a program provides service to a large or important body of users. It works by defining subgroups of the total population served and describing needs that each subgroup perceives itself to have which an institution can meet. Just as the goals and objectives were written on the basis of the library's knowledge about the needs of the population it serves, so particular programs or objectives may be focused on specific subgroups. Market segmentation is a way to analyze the population as subgroups to which specialized service may be provided.

The market, in business, is the aggregate demand of the potential buyers for a product or service. An aggregate demand is a composite of the individual demands of all potential buyers of the service.[3] Thus a target market is a homogeneous group of people to whom an organization wishes to appeal. The concept of market segmentation is based on the fact that markets, rather than being homogeneous, are actually heterogeneous—no two users are identical. However, large groups of potential users share certain characteristics of distinctive significance to marketing, and each such group constitutes a market segment. It becomes significant for library administrators to define and understand the various markets or audiences which the library serves in order to achieve utmost effectiveness.[4] This involves selecting specific audiences for specific programs, rather than attempting to be all things to all people. It can mean that you look at all possible market segments and concentrate on those segments with highest potential response to your services.

Market segmentation allows the library to group present or potential users into segments on the basis of individual differences and group similarities. It also helps libraries to identify hard nonusers. Frequently a library finds that one or two segments of its market receive primary attention, while other segments that might respond, if offered an interesting product, are being ignored. Looking at market segmentation forces us to think out appropriate strategies for reaching each group.

Libraries may segment their market in a variety of ways. Ages, special interests, and research in different subjects, for example, each provide different dimensions for segmenting a market. In delineating user groups, such questions are important:

> Is there a distinct group which has a need for the proposed services?
> How large is the group?
> How diverse is the segment?
> Are there segments in the service area which should be given a higher priority than other segments?
> Is the service area's composition stable?[5]

The diagram shown in figure 1 may be helpful in identifying the segments of the market that a public library services.

An exhaustive list of variables from Kotler's *Marketing for Nonprofit Organizations*, which librarians may use for segmenting their market, is given in figure 2. All of these variables can be applied to each of the target groups shown in figure 1. Some of the "psychographic" factors you may find in the list may lead you to seek outside expertise. Perhaps your board of trustees

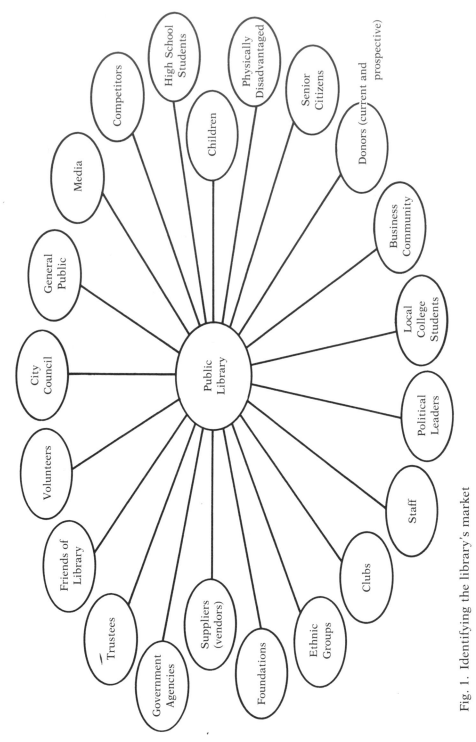

Fig. 1. Identifying the library's market

Variables	Typical breakdowns
Geographic	
Region	Pacific, Mountain, West North Central, West South Central, East North Central, East South Central, South Atlantic, Middle Atlantic, New England
County size	A, B, C, D
City or SMSA size	Under 5,000, 5,000–19,999, 20,000–49,999, 50,000–99,999, 100,000–249,999; 250,000–499,999, 500,000–999,999, 1,000,000–3,999,999, 4,000,000 or over
Density	Urban, suburban, rural
Climate	Northern, southern
Demographic	
Age	Under 6, 6–11, 12–17, 18–34, 35–49, 50–64, 65 +
Sex	Male, female
Family size	1–2, 3–4, 5 +
Family life cycle	Young, single; young, married, no children; young, married, youngest child under six; young, married, youngest child six or over; older, married, with children; older, married, no children under 18; older, single; other
Income	Under $5,000, $5,000–$7,999, $8,000–$9,999, over $10,000
Occupation	Professional and technical; managers, officials and proprietors; clerical, sales; craftsmen, foremen; operatives; farmers, retired; students; housewives; unemployed
Education	Grade school or less; some high school; graduated high school; some college; graduated college
Religion	Catholic, Protestant, Jewish, other
Race	White, black, Oriental [Asian]
Nationality	American, British, French, German, Eastern European, Scandinavian, Italian, Latin American, Middle Eastern, Japanese
Social class	Lower-lower, upper-lower, lower-middle, middle-middle, upper-middle, lower-upper, upper-upper
Psychographic	
Life-style	Swinger, status seeker, plain Joe
Personality	Compulsive, gregarious, authoritarian, ambitious
Benefits sought	Economy, convenience, prestige
User status	Nonuser, ex-user, potential user, first-time user, regular user
Usage rate	Light user, medium user, heavy user
Loyalty status	None; medium; strong; absolute
Readiness stage	Unaware, aware, informed, interested, desirous, intending to buy
Marketing-factor sensitivity	Quality, price, service, advertising, sales promotion

Fig. 2. Major segmentation variables and their typical breakdowns.

Philip Kotler, *Marketing for Nonprofit Organizations*, 2nd ed., p. 220. © 1982 by Prentice-Hall, Inc. Reprinted by permission of Prentice-Hall, Inc., Englewood Cliffs, N.J.

would be a good resource; perhaps the situation warrants consulting an outside market research company. In most cases, much of the information needed can be garnered from the most recent census. School and college curricula also may be used to identify needs of special groups of students. Conversations with faculty will indicate research interests, and knowledge of the parent organization as well as specific research concerns will indicate some of the target markets of a special library.

Morris Massey has suggested a unique approach for libraries to use to segment their markets. The following paraphrased examples indicate the benefits which each group (segment) receives:

The toilers need specific information or materials, are often students who must use the facilities, need quiet to some extent, require good light, would like refreshments available for breaks, prefer comfortable chairs.

The lonely hearts need social contact, like to talk, and therefore resent "cold shoulders" and quiet rules.

The searchers are project-oriented—for instance, frantic about the family tree, want information about a specific topic, need special assistance, may not be regular users, need reproduction/copy machines, need areas to spread out, are in a hurry.

The escapists are people looking for personal fantasy; new materials are most important to them.

The uninformed are not frequent users, but should be, are not familiar with facilities (guide books and large signs would help), are young people seeking answers to personal questions, probably intimidated by the librarian.[6]

Another breakdown of the market into its publics also may assist a library to set its goals and identify its major target groups—its publics. The library's publics may be classified as external, internal, collegial, and competition. Among the external publics are:

Users

Supporters (Friends of the Library, other special interest groups, etc.)

Suppliers (vendors, information brokers, consortia members, etc.)

Regulators (American Library Association, Special Library Association, Medical Library Association, etc.)

Community users (media organizations, political organizations, etc.)

The internal publics include:

Governing body (board members—prospective, current,
past; advisory council, etc.)
Employees (professional, nonprofessional, unions, etc.)
Administrators (library, city/county, university, etc.)
Volunteers

The collegial publics and competition include:

Other library providers: school, public, special, academic
Independent consultants
Information brokers
State agency
Library educational institutions

PERCEIVED BENEFITS AND THE MARKET SEGMENT

Effective marketing is always user-oriented, not seller-
oriented. It is essential to determine what benefits the target
audience will see in the offering. One application of this marketing principle to libraries is in the area of book selection. Do we
select those items which we feel are "good reading," or do we
ask customers for their ideas? There must be ongoing study and
awareness of the attitudes and interests of the public or the
library won't be used.

Whether real or imagined, the benefits the target audience
thinks that it receives should be discovered. The story hour may
be viewed by the library as a program for children but perceived as an hour of free babysitting by the mothers. Having
several copies of best sellers may be viewed by staff as a benefit
to users, but being put on a long reserve list (because the copies
are always out) could be perceived by the user as a nonbenefit,
since it is inconvenient to wait several days or weeks for the
wanted item. The perceptions of reality are as important as the
reality itself, and an effective marketing program always considers both the perception and the reality.

MARKET RESEARCH

The successful library program starts with the market research
required for analyzing marketing opportunities. The analysis
includes size and type of market, user characteristics, and those

elements that persuade or influence people to come in: brochures, advertising, personal selling, word of mouth, and past experience. Here are a few basic market research questions:

What do you want to know?
Why do you want to know?
How will you proceed to know?
Now that you know, what will you do next?
Who else, besides you, should know?
How will you communicate what you know?

Volumes have been written about methodology for data collection, including on-site observations, audits, surveys (a library favorite), the Delphi technique, and questionnaires. My favorite starting place for market research is very simple: try to find your library in the telephone book! Then make a telephone call to the library. What "image" does the switchboard operator convey? Or the recording? Is the tape up-to-date? Are the hours convenient? Can you understand the name of your library? Does the person speak too rapidly? How long are you left on "hold"?

THE MARKETING MIX

The design of an appropriate marketing program consists of analyzing marketing opportunities, identifying and selecting target markets, and developing an appropriate "marketing mix" for each audience or target market. A marketing mix is comprised of:

The product or service(s)
Promotion or communication
Channels of distribution
Price or cost

Too often the public equates marketing with only one of its tools, such as advertising or public relations (promotion). However, all of the tools or techniques included in the marketing mix must be considered when looking at a library marketing program.

Products.
Library products include *materials* (books, films, discs, educational games, videotapes, toys, framed prints, etc.), *sources*, (assistance to users, manual and computer searches, provision

of information and instruction in the use of the library, etc., and
programs (films, exhibits demonstrations, story hours, etc.). It is
important to list all of your library's "products" in order to
appeal to as many market segments as is feasible.

Promotion.
Promotion uses all of the tools of public relations—persuasive
communication, advertising, personal selling, publicity, and
incentives. The purposes of promotion are: to communicate, to
convince, and to compete. Devise and utilize creative ways to
promote your library's products and services.

In your promotion or marketing communications efforts, you
may find the following checklist helpful in designing a brochure
about a service:

Who are present and potential clients (users) in this market?
What are their needs? Are these *their* needs, based on re-
   search, or what we think they need?
Do they recognize their needs?
Where are the users located?
Can we reach them with our message?
Do we use our jargon or their language?
(This is where an effective public relations program comes
   in!)
Which of their needs are we serving now?
Why shouldn't they go somewhere else? Is the local bookstore
   more convenient, more accessible, easier to use?

If your publications are not shaped by answers to the questions
in this checklist, they are probably not as effective as they could
be.

The most effective way to promote any library is through a
personable, courteous, efficient, and knowledgeable staff.
Everyone who works in a library is considered by the public to
be a "librarian." Public service personnel must be good sales-
persons. This includes the pages who shelve books and the
library technicians, as well as the professional and administrative staff. When selecting and training library personnel, be
sure to stress that this is a profession of service to people. Never
hesitate to approach a "customer" and ask if you may help him
or her. If you don't know the answer to a customer's question,
offer to get someone who may be able to offer assistance. And
keep smiling!

Distribution.

Distribution, the third component of the marketing mix, involves getting the product or service to the users or potential users. This might involve books-by-mail, bookmobiles, storefront libraries and branches in shopping centers, as well as telephone reference service. Instead of having all people come to the main library building, an effort is made to take the books to the people. A public library has to consider the best means of making materials and services available to the public. Satellites, cable television, and other new technologies are providing challenges to librarians to deliver information more efficiently. Academic libraries must also decide whether one main collection serves faculty and students better than branch libraries that provide in-depth coverage by subject, and thus appeal more directly to special user groups (market segments).

Pricing.

Pricing often has been overlooked or ignored by libraries because they traditionally did not charge for lending books or providing services, nor were they in a competitive market, as the services they offered usually were not provided anywhere else. It may be time to take a new look at that idea. Information brokers and consultants are charging substantial fees for their services, while simultaneously using the "free" materials available in libraries. Most libraries charge a fee to the user for performing computer searches, but do not charge the user for time spent doing manual searches or for the computer time used in technical services. Fines are charged for overdue books, and clients may be charged for interlibrary loan service. Many libraries do not cost out their indirect services, and only attempt to recover a portion of their direct costs. In the case of a new service, such as information retrieval from computerized data bases, there may be no experience upon which to base a cost, and estimates are highly subjective. Some practical questions may help in your consideration of pricing:

1. To what extent are prices based on cost, demand, competition?
2. What would the likely response of user demand be to charging for some services that are now free? To raising or lowering existing fees? To eliminating existing fees?
3. How do library users psychologically interpret fees?

SUMMARY

Marketing places a great emphasis on measuring the needs and desires of each target market. It is an ongoing process. In order to remain viable, a library must provide for periodic audits of its objectives, resources, and opportunities. It must reexamine its purpose, its programs, its target groups, its environment—both external and internal—and its communication channels. Finally, it must evaluate the major marketing activities, specifically its products, pricing, distribution, personal contact, publicity, and promotion. If your library has not done this, or does not do it well, then your clients are apt to be poorly served, a situation that can result in bad word-of-mouth publicity and lack of support.

The benefits of a marketing program for a library include improved public service, due to the increased focus on the needs and interests of the various target groups served by the library; and improved efficiency in reaching the goals of the library through the systematic review that the marketing program encourages.

NOTES

1. Philip Kotler, *Marketing for Nonprofit Organizations* (Englewood Cliffs, N.J.: Prentice-Hall, 1975), p. 5.

2. Ibid.

3. Edward Cundiff, Richard Still, and Norman Govoni, *Fundamentals of Modern Marketing* (Englewood Cliffs, N.J.: Prentice-Hall, 1973).

4. Ronald J. Fryzel, "Marketing Nonprofit Institutions," *Hospital and Health Services Administration* 9: 8–16 (1978); Kotler, *Marketing*, p. 7.

5. Jo Ann Bell, *Library Management Marketing* (Chicago: Medical Library Assn., 1978), p. 11.

6. Morris Massey, "Market Analysis and Audience Research for Libraries," *Library Trends* 24: 473–91 (January, 1976).

See also:

Ralph M. Gaedeke, *Marketing in Private and Public Nonprofit Organizations* (Santa Monica, Calif.: Goodyear Publishing Co., 1977).

Patrick J. Montana, *Marketing in Nonprofit Organizations* (New York: Amacom, 1978).

Diana C. Proeschel

The Future of
Library Public Relations

All public institutions have some form of public relations, whether they do or do not recognize them. The institution's activities are continuously open to public scrutiny, and unless they are understood, respected, and appreciated by the community, the effectiveness of the institution can be jeopardized. Libraries as institutions need to respond to the total community as its constituency and make sure the desires and aspirations of the community are included in the library's decision-making process. No library can achieve its goal if it is not conscious of its public function. It will fulfill this mandate if it engages in responsible and effective public relations activities.

All too often public relations has been considered an unnecessary task for libraries. "P.R." sounds casual, almost frivolous. Its practitioners are scorned as lightweight, nice to have around upon occasion, but a bit much for the long haul. Too often public relations has been function by afterthought, with programs or publicity efforts tolerated only if there was an "artistic" staff member or if repeated requests were received from users. If practiced at all, the results were all too often clumsy, poorly thought out and executed, resulting in negative or no public impact. Thereupon, administrators would go back to their "real" world of librarianship—automation, management, etc.—saying "See, I told you so . . . that kind of thing will never work here." These reservations about public relations are unfortunate, especially since there is good reason to believe the development of sensitive and knowledgeable P.R. activities can be legitimate help to an institution seeking a mutuality of interest with other elements in its community.

Recently it has become apparent to many librarians that major P.R. efforts are essential in the fierce competition for the shrinking funds of the institutions that support them. Although we librarians have few natural enemies, neither do we have many natural supporters. As Frank J. Dempsey, director of the Arlington Heights, Illinois, Memorial Library, said at an ALA Conference program:

> Librarians must intensify their efforts to demonstrate to all citizens the basic human needs they can help to meet (information, recreation, education) and convince the large body of the nonusers that libraries can be an important element of their 'survival kit' in an increasingly complex society. This 'awareness training' is and must continue to be a major public information goal for all kinds of libraries.

A varied public relations program, enthusiastically presented on a continuing basis, can go a long way toward getting total support and widespread community interest. If people in the community become aware of every service available in the library, they will use it to its fullest advantage, with the results accruing to both the public and the library. This kind of public relations is here to stay and grow. Being in tune with society may very well even be a matter of survival, as today's users become tomorrow's legislators.

Public relations ranks in importance with other management functions such as production, distribution, and finance. More courses and seminars are being taught on public relations across the nation at the decision-making level, and on the basis of these comments I would speculate on public relations in the 1980s as follows:

Public relations will be a management function, given attention and authority at the top level. The true purpose of P.R. will be understood by management, volunteers, and staff, who will give it internal support.

There will be an integrated long term P.R. plan. Public relations practitioners will be committed to the year-after-next and beyond, finding the future irrevocably proscribed by the present.

Public relations will be conducted in the language of management, using resource allocation, crisis time management, and all the latest buzz words. The public relations practitioner will become a manager and a pragmatic counsel to top management, more responsible to and identified with operations. He or she will be equipped to devise the institution's response to change, knowing both the immediate trade-offs and the long term welfare of the institution and that of the dependent public. The risk for public relations is that as it becomes more visible, it also becomes more vulnerable and more accountable; its reward is to become a more powerful component in shaping corporate and social history.

Public relations will be more cost-oriented, with a consolidated budget, so that management will know how much they are spending for the results they see. Measurement of effectiveness will be related to cost. Skill in measurement and evaluation techniques will be necessary for future P.R. specialists. These techniques will be in a form, the results of which will retain professional validity, yet be relevant to management. This is required if tomorrow's practice is to escape its label of "fuzziness" and "softness" in the operational area, and become effective and respected in the real world of management.

Public relations managers will be better educated as P.R. expands from being merely a set of skills. Academic programs will include sophisticated behavioral science applications that will improve the practice of public relations and in-depth management skills. Public relations teaching in universities will emphasize social science research. Psychologists, psychological testing, and perception surveys will be used increasingly to learn what our problems are and how we can overcome them. Research will become an essential rather than occasional management tool and will be used effectively and resourcefully in supporting public relations concerns and recommendations. There will also be more sharing of that research to build a viable fund of knowledge. More P.R. courses and seminars will be offered by library schools as librarians realize them to be part of professional training.

More publicity will be centrally produced. Small libraries, institutions, and companies will be able to maintain the same standard of excellence as the largest institution. Systems will consolidate their resources for centralized production of publicity items and help in planning total P.R. packages. Inhouse P.R. efforts will be supplemented by outside firms that can offer expertise for special projects.

Publicity will be slicker and more professional. Visual communication will be immeasurably advanced by 3D photography, improved color film, high speed cameras, and instantaneous development and printing. These and other technological advances will produce more polished visuals. Electronic science will advance public relations to an extent unrealized today. There will be more training in planning and editing for the spoken word; the speaking platform, radio, television, film, cable TV, audio and video tapes and discs will become the dominant media for communications. There will be more structuring for the face-to-face group encounter, and the public relations practitioner will assert an initiative in programming for such dialogues.

How do we as librarians get a head start on public relations for the 1980s? Learn the language of management. Be able to show how budget cuts will adversely affect services. Show the impact if resources become more limited. Quantify possible benefits of your programs. Continually evaluate your programs and pass feedback to management. Have checkpoints for evaluation as the program progresses; do not wait until it is completed. Do a survey to find out how well you are doing. Public relations takes patience, persistence, and tenacity. It is also an occupation in which you never stop learning. You have the resources and talent to think of and carry out ideas that are appealing to the community. The truth about libraries is a good story, and you can tell that story and have fun in the telling.

Ann Heidbreder Eastman

Making Common Cause: Libraries and Their Allies

It is appropriate that the American Library Association (ALA) and its affiliates be the prime movers in promoting libraries, but valuable opportunities are lost if ALA is viewed as the *only* organization in the library/information science/reading/books field. We have many other strong and natural allies with whom we can jointly launch campaigns, conduct projects, generate proposals and funding, and the like. The "explosion" of attention to public relations during Betty Stone's presidency, culminating in the 1982 annual conference in Philadelphia, will pay out most handsomely, it seems to me, if those of us concerned about the future of libraries in our society look outside the library profession for additional allies.

Two examples of past successes help to make this point. National Library Week (NLW) itself was started not by ALA but by the National Book Committee, a citizens group founded in 1954 to combat censorship and other threats to library development. The deputy director of ALA helped to staff the steering committee—comprised of professionals from the media, corporations, publishing houses, as well as libraries—and generated NLW participation through ALA committees and staff. The Knapp School Library Development project, administered by ALA, grew out of an NLW story in *Parade*.

The second example is the Educational Media Selection Centers (EMSC) project sponsored by the National Book Committee. It was governed by the first comprehensive consortium of education and library organizations that actually *worked* together on a project (a former president of ALA remarked, not just in jest, that if the EMSC project did nothing else—and it did—it got school administrators, business officers, classroom teachers, and librarians talking seriously with one another in the same room!).

Support for the National Book Committee dwindled and it closed in 1974, but there are other groups that share goals with librarians. Library supporters may accomplish more if they can encourage nonlibrary groups to join in promoting appropriate aspects of library service. It is, after all, not a matter of libraries for the sake of libraries but libraries for the people they serve. ALA and libraries are at the center of any library P.R. program, but non-ALA organizations move around them.

WHO ARE LIBRARY ALLIES?

Very close to ALA are other national professional library and information science organizations (for example, the Special Libraries Association, the Medical Library Association), the National Commission on Libraries and Information Science, the Center for the Book in the Library of Congress. There are also publisher and information-producer associations such as the Association of American Publishers (AAP), the Children's Book Council (CBC), and the Information Industries Association (IIA). ALA often joins with such organizations in giving voice to the library and information science position on issues before Congress and other governmental agencies. Occasionally, the AAP and the CBC have sponsored conferences and seminars jointly with librarians, but no continuous effort has been made to involve groups in this category in planning for library public information.

Like the National Book Committee, the Center for the Book is composed of an advisory board of citizens—in this case, primarily scholars, publishers, and booksellers—and librarians. The center sponsored an effective library promotion project called "Books Make a Difference," about which more will be said later.

There is another group of organizations, mostly educational, whose members also deal in the written and spoken word—the American Booksellers Association, the International Reading Association, Literacy Volunteers of America, the Modern Language Association, the National Council of Teachers of English, to name a few. All are concerned about reading and literacy in America. They have their own organizational structures and conferences, where libraries as social institutions are not an important topic. They do, however, feature programs about books, authors, and the lifetime reading habit. They might not respond to "support your local library" campaigns but they will be interested in projects about reading, books, and authors because that's where they live, too.

Most of the organizations in these categories have local, state, or regional units within reach of every library promoter in the country. If you approach your state teachers of English association or state reading council *assuming* that they share your enthusiasm for a reading campaign, very likely they will.

Slightly more remote from the library are organizations such as the American Association of University Women, General Federation of Women's Clubs, League of Women Voters, Kiwanis, Lions, Rotary, Zonta and other community and service groups. Many—for example, Boy Scouts and Girl Scouts—focus on reading or library use in a particular way. Most women's organizations have book discussion groups. The League of Women Voters is always interested in the library needs of a community and in books and other materials about issues they are studying, the political process, women and the law, etc. Men's service clubs often support local programs and projects for children and youth who have reading problems or lack access to good children's books. ALA makes contact with these organizations, too, at the national level, but local library supporters should talk often and enthusiastically with local officers and committee chairs to learn what the local group is doing that the library can support. Later, when there is a library promotion campaign in the making, the library knows who may respond, and how.

Many groups of citizens have already been mobilized to one degree or another on behalf of libraries—Friends of local libraries, Friends of Libraries U.S.A., trustees, the more than 50,000 citizens who participated in the pre-White House Conference process and the White House Conference on Library and Information Services (WHCLIS) itself, members of National Citizens for Public Libraries, past and present members of the National Commission on Library and Information Science and its numerous task forces, and past and present members of the Center for the Book Advisory Board, to name a few. Some states have put their WHCLIS citizen delegates to work on statewide P.R. programs; many have not. Some organizations—including Friends of Libraries U.S.A., the American Library Trustee Asso-

Ann Heidbreder Eastman

ciation and the Friends, Volunteers and Advocates Committee of the Public Relation Section of ALA—communicate effectively with the members.

Other organizations, including, alas, some state library associations, do no more than solicit members and send an occasional newsletter. Nonlibrarians are included on committees and programs only as tokens, if at all. The "information" being beamed to the "public," in this case, is that no matter what the lay person's expertise professionally, the library group doesn't need it.

Numerous state associations have, in contrast, reached out to lay people by asking them to work as equal partners with librarians on tasks that need to be done; among these are California, Florida, Illinois, Maryland, Minnesota, New York, Pennsylvania, and South Carolina. My message here is: If you are going to make second-class citizens of lay association members, don't pretend to involve them in the first place. You'll do more harm than good.

The organizations that have announced the goal of mobilizing citizen support for libraries are, however, so numerous that the dedicated lay group is being fragmented. We simply cannot be active members of all of them. Perhaps the time has come for some agency to organize a national *coordinating* council of groups attempting to involve citizens in library public information. The council would gather information about public relations plans of member organizations and disseminate it, and it would also plan major national campaigns that the member organizations would support.

Some might view the ALA as the appropriate organization to organize such a council. It could function well as an adjunct to the Public Information Office (PIO). Since the staff of the PIO gathers information about all kinds of library public information activities, they function informally in a coordinating capacity now.

But other groups, especially those in which citizen library supporters are most active, might view ALA sponsorship as an attempt to assure that the work of member library support groups conformed to the plans and policies of ALA. Furthermore, often the approach of library supporters is strengthened when they can report, especially to legislators, that they speak not for the library profession but for library *users*.

Perhaps the National Commission on Libraries and Information Science could establish a task force to investigate the need for a coordinating council. The task force could gather information about what library support groups are doing now, meet with staff members and chairs of the affected groups, and recommend the kind of national network to be created to share information, avoid duplication, and plan effectively what contribution the individual groups could make to a broad-based yet focused library P.R. program.

Representatives of individual organizations would need to be informed about the plans and policies of their respective organizations so as to discuss effectively appropriate public relations efforts. A major national campaign planned by the coordinating council would not be so confined to the goals of any one organization that it did not benefit most or all of the others. The council also could encourage state and local units of national organizations to work together on particular campaigns.

PUBLIC RELATIONS WITHOUT TURF

Two ingredients are essential to the success of such a saturation library public relations effort: (1) intellectual pursuit of the notion that the tools of public relations can be used to accomplish a change of attitude about some aspect of library service, and (2) genuine commitment to the setting aside of "turf" considerations. ALA and many other publishers provide publications that tell the library profession how to "do" public relations but little exists that helps us learn how to think about public relations goals and ways to reach them. Public relations efforts that float off unattached to serious thought end up being nice posters, cute brochures, snappy spots, but public relations cannot be detached from the serious facts of life libraries face today nor can P.R. people be out of the direct line of communication with library directors and other administrators. They need to be involved as managers in solving library problems. The approach should be "This is our problem. How are we going to solve it?" rather than "Write a release and do a poster for this (isolated, one-shot) program."

The question of turf is complicated. Nonprofit, membership organizations in particular need to make visible their work on behalf of dues-payers if they expect to thrive. Common sense and the success records of past efforts, however, tell us that numerous nonlibrary organizations share the concerns of librarians for the learning/reading/access-to-information welfare of users. Moreover, it is unnecessary to claim an area as exclusively one's own in order to gain a public image of one's work in that area; witness ALA's work over the years with the Adult Education Association, the American National Standards Institute, the International Reading Association, and the Rural Education Association, to name a few.

The National Book Committee and the Center for the Book also are representative of non-ALA groups that bring librarians together with publishers, scholars, and library users to work on projects of benefit to all parties. One of the most recent—and promising—of ALA's efforts in this area is the new Coalition for Literacy, which will focus national attention and resources on adult literacy. Joining ALA are some of the organizations named above and the American Association of Advertising Agencies (AAAA), B. Dalton Booksellers, Laubach Literacy International, Literacy Volunteers of America, and the National Commission on Libraries and Information Science.

A DECLARATION OF LIBRARY INTERDEPENDENCE

The philosophical base from which such effective cooperation derives is the question, "What can we do together to solve this problem," not "What help can I get from related organizations to do my thing?" Those are two quite different approaches, and usually the first succeeds while the second does not. Even if the primary ideas are put forward by one group, all need to get some of the credit. Furthermore, a certain kind and degree of *acknowledged* theft isn't a bad idea. If a good idea has worked somewhere else and can be adapted to the promotion of libraries, why not use it—assuming you have the permission (and perhaps the support) of the originator?

In her ALA presidential address, Carol Nemeyer called upon libraries to join her in "a new library declaration of interdependence" with business, other library and information organizations, political activists for allied groups, publishers associations, and the White House Conference on Library and Information Services Taskforce (WHCLIST) and concluded this part of her speech by saying,

> We have the opportunity to move ahead aggressively, linked together and to our nonlibrarian friends and colleagues to secure the place for libraries in this puzzling environment of unprecedented fiscal and professional flux.

Building on President Betty Stone's emphasis on public awareness of libraries, Ms. Nemeyer said,

> We must effectively speak out on behalf of libraries. Proudly, without embarrassment we must continue to increase awareness of libraries. Libraries enhance the productivity of industry and enrich the lives of all who use them. I can think of no business or industry that does not benefit by a literate and well-informed populace.

THE BOOKS MAKE A DIFFERENCE PROJECT

One of the most effective library/books/reading promotion efforts to be launched recently is the "Books Make a Difference" project, an interview project sponsored by the Center for the Book in the Library of Congress and the College of Arts and Sciences at Virginia Tech. Work began when the center's Reading Development Committee wanted to do something that would bring the center, the Library of Congress, and libraries in general to the attention of the public. It was decided that we would send capable interviewers to a variety of locales in this country to ask two questions: What book made the greatest difference in your life? and, What was that difference?

Over 1,300 people in forty-four states were asked these questions between July, 1980, and March, 1981. More than 500 of these responses were tape recorded. Gordon A. Sabine, on leave of absence from his position as professor of journalism at Virginia Tech, was the interviewer, assisted by his wife, Patricia. I am a member of the center's executive committee and am the project coordinator. Like all Center for the Book projects, the "Books Make a Difference" effort was funded by private contributions from individuals and organizations.

How Do Books Make a Difference?

The Sabines found that reading was an intensely personal and individual experience. There was no way to predict which book would be named or what difference it would make, or even if it would be a *book* that provided the most influential reading experience. Occasionally, it was a magazine article, a newspaper story, or a report. Responses showed that people read for every reason: for pleasure, to find a job, for knowledge, to have something to talk about, for inspiration, for information, and out of curiosity. No single book dominated, although the Bible was named by about five percent of the respondents. Only four other books were mentioned more than three times and when they were, just as with the Bible, the difference they had made varied widely among individuals. The four books were *The Autobiography of Benjamin Franklin, Atlas Shrugged* by Ayn Rand, *The Boy Scout Handbook,* and the dictionary. Bestsellers were not named very often, and neither were classics. In more than one instance, the satisfaction gained from reading an entire book for the first time made that book the most significant one in a person's life.

Public Information

Coverage of the "Books Make a Difference" project in the media has been extraordinary. Librarians in places where the Sabines interviewed called and wrote to local papers, where they were interviewed about the project and about the books being named in the locality. Several columnists started regular features about books and the differences they made, which are still going on. Hosts of call-in talk shows have found the "Books Make a Difference" concept to be popular; broadcasters started by interviewing the Sabines and continued by interviewing local residents. Susan Stamberg interviewed Gordon Sabine for "All Things Considered" on National Public Radio. Two weeks later she did segments on two days featuring the books, differences, and voices of listeners from across the country. During her speech in Philadelphia in 1982, she cited this project as representative of the kind of effective work broadcasters and librarians can do together.

One public library has worked out a way to let television viewers know that books make a difference. As a result of participation in this project, a local television celebrity on a weekly magazine show in Spokane, Washington, calls the library when he thinks viewers might want to learn more about a particular item. The library staff suggests several titles. Titles are shown with the suggestion that interested people can find them at their local public library. While this scenario sounds like a spinoff of the Center for the Book/CBS "Read More about It" effort, it grew out of the Sabines' visit.

In May, 1983, Library Professional Publications, an imprint of the Shoe String Press, published *Books That Made the Difference: What People Told Us* by Gordon A. and Patricia L. Sabine. Included are fifty pages of how-to-do-it for local projects—including very practical advice about recruiting a professional interviewer, organizing the project, and ways to use the statements about books and differences in promoting libraries, especially in demonstrating that books and libraries are important to people.

At a Library Administration and Management Association (LAMA) program in Los Angeles (1983), representatives of the Public Relations Section of LAMA, Public Library Association, Chief Officers of Library Agencies, and WHCLIS discussed ways libraries can plan and conduct their own local "Books Make a Difference" projects. WHCLIST is preparing a proposal for major funding to have prominent people and the not-so-prominent interviewed and to use their books and differences as a springboard for local library programming.

The "Books Make a Difference" project could not have been done without the support and help of good librarians. It was initiated, however, by one of those non-ALA organizations that serves as a catalyst for many individuals, organizations, and agencies that are dedicated to the welfare of libraries and the importance of books and reading in our society. This project is a good example of the kind of effort that works both ways: it helps to communicate the needs and interests of a community to its library, and it takes word about the library into the community.

WHERE DO I START?

Local libraries are not the Library of Congress, and local library supporters are not the famous authors, publishers, scholars, and librarians on the Center for the Book Advisory Board. However, P.R.-minded librarians can find allies in their communities. One need not wait for a national organization to identify them. There are far more local organizations and units of national groups for librarians to work with than there are national groups.

The first thing the library staff must do is (this will sound familiar) *define goals.* In the library P.R. area, this means deciding what it is you want to accomplish. Goals can be specific or general, short- or long-term. Most effective librarians are working on a number of goals at the same time. One may be to draw a particular group into the library for programs and services— the elderly, for instance. Another might be to make users comfortable with using a computer terminal, rather than a card catalog, to find books and other materials. A third might be to gather and organize new data for the town council, which will soon be considering your budget request. Work on one of these doesn't stop when work on another starts.

If one of your goals is to attract senior citizens to your library, the allies in your community are the agencies that serve that age group and the organizations to which they belong. Such agencies are the social services department of the local hospital, the social security office, the senior citizens center, the visiting nurses association, Meals on Wheels, the local medical association; appropriate organizations would include the local unit of the American Association of Retired People (AARP) and groups of retirees from various fields.

In the small town where I grew up, if you want to find active retirees with good ideas and time to devote to them, you have luncheon on Wednesday at the Elks Club so you can talk with the members of the "Do Nothing Club" while they eat and play bridge. No officers, no dues, no paperwork—but a great deal of energy and an impressive record of service in their community.

Having identified the appropriate groups, one would go to see the staff members and leaders in these groups to find out what their goals and programs are and to explain how they would be enhanced and strengthened by some aspect of library service— book exhibits or discussions, for example, or service to retirement and nursing homes, programs in the library about finding part-time jobs in the community, filing tax returns, or travel. People outside the library know what senior citizens want and need from the community; librarians know how their services and resources help to fill those needs. Someone is needed to make the "connection," and that person is the local librarian.

Not all the librarians in a local library can belong to all the community organizations but, within reason, library professionals should be encouraged to put their personal tastes, talents, and inclinations to work for the library. If you're trying to increase your contacts with community leaders, go where they are. Consider joining Zonta, Altrusa, Rotary, Kiwanis, and other service and civic organizations. Librarians who like to garden might join the local garden club (women who garden often have houses; homeowners pay taxes—the bigger the house and garden, the higher the taxes). If you attended a college or university that has a local alumni group, go to the meetings, become an active member. An obvious choice for librarians would be book, reading, and drama groups.

What you are doing, in fact, is identifying the power base in your community and getting to know it while its members get to know you. Once you have made these contacts and participated in the group's work, you will begin to understand what kinds of projects appeal to which groups. In the future, whether you are trying to get out a crowd for a visiting author, to interest a particular group in planning a joint program on a topic of community interest, or to acquaint people with the services you already are providing—services you know the community needs but cannot afford, these groups will help lobby for additional funds for the library, and you will know where to turn for help.

Newspaper, radio, and television personnel are very important to a successful library public relations effort. One's first inclination is to get to know the reporters and broadcasters who actually deliver the news, features, and columns, who moderate talk shows, interview people with interesting stories to tell. They are important and elsewhere in this book you will find information about approaching them, informing them, keeping them interested—working effectively with them. But don't overlook the people these individuals work for—the owners and managers of local papers and stations. These are the people you want to invite to serve on advisory and project committees, to meet with the staff, and, perhaps, some members of the board who are especially interested in working with community groups and in library public relations. Ask their advice openly about ways to better inform the community. As those who manage the communications media have responded to such requests for help and advice, they have been known to volunteer to have spots made, hold space for a library column, assign people to cover library and library-related events.

WHAT HAPPENS NEXT?

What happens next is up to you. Once you have made effective contacts and dedicated the necessary time to cultivating them—as well as your knowledge of the work of allied groups—you should decide the best time to propose the project you have in mind. Most organized groups plan programs and other activities in advance so spring and summer are good times to take your ideas to meetings, make suggestions, identify other groups and individuals who would be interested in what you are pro-posing. Often it is wise to try out an idea on several individuals on the board or committee before presenting it to the entire group. This plan allows you to better tailor your suggestion to the group as a whole and, incidentally, to "defuse" someone who might object publicly. If you hear and respond to negative comments in private, you may not have to handle them in the meeting. Often people who appear to be negative are simply uninformed—and unwilling to admit that before a group.

It is likely that every jointly sponsored program or project reflects compromises arrived at during the planning stages. Librarians cannot expect other professionals to view proposals exactly as librarians do. For one thing, a cosponsoring organiza-tion is likely to want to see some reflection of its work in the final plan. Expect to make some changes in the idea you are present-ing and be flexible when they are suggested. Altering your ideas in the right way at the right time could spell success, not failure, for the enterprise. Remember that the cosponsor probably knows how the anticipated audience will react. Furthermore, the cosponsor will want the project to help fulfill a goal of the nonlibrary organization, as well as the goal of the library.

One effective way to generate enthusiasm for a jointly spon-sored project is to suggest that it have an advisory committee or planning committee on which representatives of both organiza-tions would sit. For some projects, a large group is not appropri-ate, but for some—especially those that are complex, are car-ried out over a long period of time, and for which a large number of participants is expected—such a committee is important. In addition to information and ideas, the project gains the support of people who know about it early on, who can talk about it in the community, and who will have, by virtue of their presence on the committee, assumed some responsibility for its success. In short, a planning or advisory committee often transforms itself into a public information support group by the end of the process. It can also be a good source of information and ideas about evaluating the project after it is over and helping the community to take the next step, if there is one.

SHARE THE WEALTH

When you have completed a successful joint project, don't stop there. Tell your community, of course, but let your professional colleagues in your state and region know of your success, with the suggestion that the state and regional library associations (1) sponsor the same project (or a variation of it appropriate for the larger area), or (2) channel information about the way you worked with a nonlibrary organization to other librarians in the state and region. The usual publicity materials about the project itself should be sent, of course, to state-based and regional publications and broadcasters so readers and viewers know *what* you did. You should write a piece that tells *how* you accomplished what you did, especially how you worked successfully with the cosponsor.

It's always tempting to promote what the library has done but in this case it doesn't hurt to be generous. Let the cosponsor have a fair share of the credit, and perhaps a bit more. If your library, the National Council of Teachers of English affiliate, the local International Reading Association council, and the College of Education in your local university have joined forces to launch a successful Literacy Volunteers of America program in your community, you don't have to insist that the idea was yours. The *news* is that all four of you combined forces to combat illiteracy.

AND YOU CALL THIS PUBLIC RELATIONS?

In the larger sense of the term, the kind of work described *is* public relations: bringing the library to the attention of its publics. It is, perhaps, helpful to think of the library's audience as a number of publics, not just one. Some of your public relations is directed to that large, general audience, but some of it can—and should—be directed to segments of that public who also are another organization's or agency's public. The message gets through with double strength—the library's and the cosponsor's.

Finally, for information about a number of successful jointly sponsored library P.R. programs, read *68 Great Ideas: The Library Awareness Handbook* published by the American Library Association. Some of these are library efforts that were promoted in concert with other organizations. Some are jointly sponsored projects. Since the descriptions are brief and readers may want to write for how-to information, names and addresses are provided.

The library community needs a continuing service of this kind; far more is going on in the field of library public relations than periodicals have space to report. In fact, *68 Great Ideas* is the kind of annual report the coordinating council mentioned earlier might be expected to make. If you are motivated to look around your community for natural allies in the cause of promoting library service, you will find the reward to be worth the effort.

The last word comes from Will Manley, an able and experienced director and promoter of libraries in Wisconsin, Illinois, and Arizona. In a recent book from Library Professional Publications (Shoe String Press) entitled *Snowballs in the Bookdrop: Talking It Over with Your Library's Community*, he states:

> Public relations, which could use an image overhaul of its own, is not packaging, publicity, press agentry, promotion, advertising, marketing, merchandising, manipulating, retailing, or displaying. It is not pamphlets, flyers, newsletters, tee-shirts, bulletin boards, slogans, or posters.
>
> Public relations is your relationship with the public, whoever "you" are: company, agency, institution or individual. Public library public relations is the relationship of your library to the public, but equally, it is the way in which the public relates to your library. Obviously the two concepts are different sides of the same coin.

Margaret Chartrand

Budgeting for a Public Relations Program

As in every other library function, planning is the number one factor influencing successful public relations. Without planning, budgeting is impossible. Therefore you must begin your budget process with planning. You will be lucky if your organization has well-articulated goals and objectives, luckier still if your library has a long-range plan. These plans will make your planning job much easier, because you can then tailor your public relations plans to meet the corporate goals and objectives.

If you are not lucky enough to be on this level of planning with your library, you should begin each planning and budgeting cycle by setting down on paper your list of objectives to be accomplished during the next twelve to eighteen months. As the initiator of these plans, you will discuss them first with your senior management and other department heads, not only to get their feedback but to get their commitment to your plans.

Once you have drawn up your new objectives and they have been accepted, it will be time to cost them out. At this point you need only estimates, rather than exact costs; your library doubtless goes through a bidding system on such items as the purchase of printed material. If you are brand new to the budgeting cycle you will need special help; any potential supplier will be happy to provide an estimate on any item.

Before you go any further with the process, review the current functions of the department, using whatever techniques your library employs for such tasks. At this point you will look at every item to see if it achieved its objective, was effective from a public relations perspective, and was cost effective. Eliminate those parts of the P.R. program that did not meet the criteria, and retain those parts that did. Now you may set your budget priorities, an invaluable step when inevitable budget cuts must be faced.

The next step is tricky for a P.R. budget. You have identified the programs required to meet the objectives; now you must translate this information into the functions of public relations, so that the accounting sheets and budget reports are easy for the auditor to understand. Since public relations is a support service, you will want to canvass all other library departments for their publications, exhibits, signage, advertising, and special events needs so that their costs may be added to your own. Knowing their needs will also be useful in planning the yearly work flow for you and your staff.

Budget headings for a P.R. department would include the following:

Staff
full time
part time
Print shop
supplies
paper
envelopes
wire
chemicals
cleanup cloths
postage
ink
printing plates
Graphics
clip art
art supplies
paper
boards
photostats
signage materials
transfer letters
photography and
typesetting equipment
Exhibits
photography

photostats
boards
art supplies
hardware supplies
Publications
posters
flyers
booklets
annual reports
newsletters
pathfinders
booklists
catalogs
stationery
business cards
forms
catalog cards
Audiovisual presentations
for promotion or staff
training
Advertising
special events
special announcements
special promotions
clipping service

Equipment, including
    maintenance contracts
Administrative expenses
  books
  periodicals
  memberships in professional
    organizations

staff training
travel
entertainment and
    refreshments for special
    events.

The large library system I work in devotes nearly three percent of its total budget to the functions listed under these categories. For the purpose of this article, we will avoid dollar figures and deal with money in percentage figures.

The recommendation would be that between one and three percent of the total library budget be expended on public relations. Using the categories indicated earlier, the breakdown for a public relations budget would look roughly like this: *staff,* 40 percent of the total public relations budget figure; *publications,* 30 percent; *equipment,* 12 percent; *graphics,* 2 percent; *press room,* 2 percent; *exhibits,* 2 percent; *audiovisuals,* 2 percent; *advertising,* 2 percent; and *administration,* 8 percent. Keeping careful control of the spending is essential and should be accomplished in the standard method of your library.

Upon completion of this budgeting process, you will have the basis of an effective, well-managed P.R. program that supports the overall goals and objectives of the library.

Diana C. Proeschel

A P.R. Checklist for Project Coordinators

The planning process for a library's public relations project can be an exciting part of the entire promotion. Organization, coupled with advice and enthusiasm from colleagues and the support of the administration, is the first step of a successful program.

Following is a checklist designed to assist in planning the P.R. program. It is based on a document used by U.S. Army base librarians in planning promotions offered to transient personnel with a wide range of interests and varying levels of education. Most P.R. project coordinators will be able to use this as a basic document, with the addition of items of direct concern to their public relations program in the sections marked "other."

	Yes	In Process	Planned	No	Not Applicable
BACKGROUND INFORMATION					
A. What sources of information were used to identify the target audience?					
Advisory committees	☐	☐	☐	☐	☐
Files	☐	☐	☐	☐	☐
Input from clubs and organizations	☐	☐	☐	☐	☐
Interviews	☐	☐	☐	☐	☐
News media (articles in newspapers and other local publications and on television news documentaries)	☐	☐	☐	☐	☐
Personal knowledge	☐	☐	☐	☐	☐
Questionnaires	☐	☐	☐	☐	☐
Staff members	☐	☐	☐	☐	☐
Surveys	☐	☐	☐	☐	☐
Other (list) _____	☐	☐	☐	☐	☐
_____	☐	☐	☐	☐	☐
_____	☐	☐	☐	☐	☐
B. Has the following information been collected about the target audience?					
Age	☐	☐	☐	☐	☐
Attitudes held about library service	☐	☐	☐	☐	☐
Education level	☐	☐	☐	☐	☐
Ethnic background	☐	☐	☐	☐	☐
Goals	☐	☐	☐	☐	☐
Interests	☐	☐	☐	☐	☐
Lifestyles	☐	☐	☐	☐	☐
Number	☐	☐	☐	☐	☐
Per capita income	☐	☐	☐	☐	☐
Perceived self-interest	☐	☐	☐	☐	☐
Sex	☐	☐	☐	☐	☐
Transience (mobility)	☐	☐	☐	☐	☐
Other (list) _____	☐	☐	☐	☐	☐
_____	☐	☐	☐	☐	☐
_____	☐	☐	☐	☐	☐

	Yes	In Process	Planned	No	Not Applicable
C. Has the following background information been collected about the library?					
Availability of supplies	□	□	□	□	□
Condition of equipment	□	□	□	□	□
Facility attractiveness	□	□	□	□	□
Internal directional signs	□	□	□	□	□
Is the building clearly marked	□	□	□	□	□
Scope of collection	□	□	□	□	□
Efficiency of arrangement	□	□	□	□	□
Traffic pattern	□	□	□	□	□
Weaknesses/strengths of collection	□	□	□	□	□
Other (list) _____	□	□	□	□	□
_____	□	□	□	□	□
_____	□	□	□	□	□
_____	□	□	□	□	□
_____	□	□	□	□	□
D. Has the following been collected about library staff?					
Administrative support	□	□	□	□	□
Amount of education/training	□	□	□	□	□
Attitudes about library service	□	□	□	□	□
Attitudes/perceptions on weaknesses and strengths of the library	□	□	□	□	□
Efficiency	□	□	□	□	□
Interest(s) of personnel	□	□	□	□	□
Knowledge of library goals	□	□	□	□	□
Length of service	□	□	□	□	□
Secretarial support	□	□	□	□	□
Talent(s) of personnel	□	□	□	□	□
Staff ideas of public expectations of library service	□	□	□	□	□
Other (list) _____	□	□	□	□	□
_____	□	□	□	□	□
_____	□	□	□	□	□
_____	□	□	□	□	□
_____	□	□	□	□	□

	Yes	In Process	Planned	No	Not Applicable
OBJECTIVE SETTING					
A. Are objectives divided into long-range and short-range goals?	□	□	□	□	□
B. Which groups assisted in the development and review of the objectives?					
Administration	□	□	□	□	□
Board	□	□	□	□	□
Department heads	□	□	□	□	□
Patrons	□	□	□	□	□
Staff	□	□	□	□	□
Volunteers	□	□	□	□	□
Other (list) _____	□	□	□	□	□
_____	□	□	□	□	□
_____	□	□	□	□	□
C. Are specific anticipated results described? For example: "percentage of increase; introduction of new services; larger . . . ; smaller . . . ;" etc.	□	□	□	□	□
D. Are the anticipated results measurable?	□	□	□	□	□
E. Are program deadlines realistic and consistent with personnel and financial resources?	□	□	□	□	□
F. Other (list) _____	□	□	□	□	□
SCHEDULE SETTING					
A. Is there a written plan for the program?	□	□	□	□	□
B. Is the plan descriptive of the responsibility, authority and accountability of each staff member?	□	□	□	□	□

	Yes	In Process	Planned	No	Not Applicable
C. Does the plan have start and end dates for the project?	□	□	□	□	□
D. Are all the major steps involved in each activity shown on the plan?	□	□	□	□	□
E. Are there start and end dates for each major step of the plan?	□	□	□	□	□
F. Are staff members assigned specific responsibilities with start and end dates?	□	□	□	□	□
G. Are necessary approval procedures scheduled?	□	□	□	□	□
H. Other (list) _____	□	□	□	□	□
_____	□	□	□	□	□
_____	□	□	□	□	□

BUDGET

	Yes	In Process	Planned	No	Not Applicable
A. Are all projected activities listed with an estimated cost?	□	□	□	□	□
B. Are expenditures and resource allocations monitored?	□	□	□	□	□
C. Does the budget provide for the following?					
Equipment	□	□	□	□	□
Graphic artist	□	□	□	□	□
Indirect costs	□	□	□	□	□
Staff	□	□	□	□	□
Photography	□	□	□	□	□
Printing	□	□	□	□	□
Purchased services	□	□	□	□	□
Repair and maintenance of equipment	□	□	□	□	□
Salaries	□	□	□	□	□
Special or miscellaneous costs	□	□	□	□	□
Supplies	□	□	□	□	□

	Yes	In Process	Planned	No	Not Applicable
Telephone	☐	☐	☐	☐	☐
Travel	☐	☐	☐	☐	☐
Other (list) _____	☐	☐	☐	☐	☐
_____	☐	☐	☐	☐	☐
_____	☐	☐	☐	☐	☐
D. Is the budget based on:					
Records of past expenditures?	☐	☐	☐	☐	☐
Anticipated work loads?	☐	☐	☐	☐	☐
E. Does the budget allow for high peaks and low points of activity?	☐	☐	☐	☐	☐
F. Is there a formalized system for maintenance of supplies for this project?	☐	☐	☐	☐	☐

SELECTION OF COMMUNICATION TECHNIQUES

	Yes	In Process	Planned	No	Not Applicable
Indicate the communication techniques which will be used:					
Conference	☐	☐	☐	☐	☐
Contests	☐	☐	☐	☐	☐
Demonstrations	☐	☐	☐	☐	☐
Exhibits	☐	☐	☐	☐	☐
Feature articles	☐	☐	☐	☐	☐
Films	☐	☐	☐	☐	☐
Fliers/handouts	☐	☐	☐	☐	☐
News releases	☐	☐	☐	☐	☐
News stories	☐	☐	☐	☐	☐
Panels	☐	☐	☐	☐	☐
Posters	☐	☐	☐	☐	☐
Public service announcements (radio and television)	☐	☐	☐	☐	☐
Receptions	☐	☐	☐	☐	☐
Seminars	☐	☐	☐	☐	☐
Slide/tape presentations	☐	☐	☐	☐	☐
Workshops	☐	☐	☐	☐	☐
Other (list) _____	☐	☐	☐	☐	☐
_____	☐	☐	☐	☐	☐
_____	☐	☐	☐	☐	☐

	Yes	In Process	Planned	No	Not Applicable
PREPARATION OF SUPPORTING MATERIALS					
A. Do the supporting materials augment and reinforce each other through their:					
Content?	☐	☐	☐	☐	☐
Literary style?	☐	☐	☐	☐	☐
Artistic design?	☐	☐	☐	☐	☐
B. Is the production schedule of support material approved and ready for use before the time needed?	☐	☐	☐	☐	☐
C. Is the shelf life of the support items indicated?	☐	☐	☐	☐	☐
D. Is the shelf life of the support items enforced?	☐	☐	☐	☐	☐
EVALUATION					
A. Planning					
Were the program objectives achieved?	☐	☐	☐	☐	☐
Were provisions made in advance for measuring results?	☐	☐	☐	☐	☐
Were these provisions adequate?	☐	☐	☐	☐	☐
Is there an overall review of the program with results measured against assigned objectives?	☐	☐	☐	☐	☐
Could the results have been more effective?	☐	☐	☐	☐	☐
Will the lesson learned be integrated into better evaluation?	☐	☐	☐	☐	☐
Were any of the following procedures used for evaluation:					
Mail campaign	☐	☐	☐	☐	☐

	Yes	In Process	Planned	No	Not Applicable
Qualitative factors	☐	☐	☐	☐	☐
Telephone surveys	☐	☐	☐	☐	☐
Research studies	☐	☐	☐	☐	☐
Other (list) _____	☐	☐	☐	☐	☐
_____	☐	☐	☐	☐	☐
_____	☐	☐	☐	☐	☐
Will a formal written report be made of the project?	☐	☐	☐	☐	☐

B. Staff

	Yes	In Process	Planned	No	Not Applicable
Did those concerned understand their jobs?	☐	☐	☐	☐	☐
Did all concerned departments/personnel cooperate?	☐	☐	☐	☐	☐
Were assignments made of the person/department that will answer inquiries and handle follow-up procedures?	☐	☐	☐	☐	☐
Did staff have an opportunity to provide recommendations/suggestions for future similar projects?	☐	☐	☐	☐	☐

C. Program

	Yes	In Process	Planned	No	Not Applicable
Was the desired publicity received before, during, and after the completion of the program?	☐	☐	☐	☐	☐
Were records kept of the following coverage:					
Impact measurement	☐	☐	☐	☐	☐
Print media	☐	☐	☐	☐	☐
Radio and television	☐	☐	☐	☐	☐
Testing (pre/post testing, if applicable)	☐	☐	☐	☐	☐
Other (list) _____	☐	☐	☐	☐	☐
_____	☐	☐	☐	☐	☐
_____	☐	☐	☐	☐	☐

	Yes	In Process	Planned	No	Not Applicable
Was there anticipation of the information the audience would request (were there enough lists, instructions, etc.)?	☐	☐	☐	☐	☐
Was the program within the budget?	☐	☐	☐	☐	☐
Could better provisions have been made for unforeseen circumstances?	☐	☐	☐	☐	☐
Were steps taken to improve future programs of the same type on the basis of the measurement of objectives?	☐	☐	☐	☐	☐

Part Two

Some
Special Audiences

*Florence Frette Stiles, Janet R. Bean,
and Virginia Baeckler*

Public Relations for the Public Library

The public library should and must work for good public relations, for two-way communication with the community. As an institution whose constituency is all the people, the public library is responsible for notifying them of the services available to them. This belief was reflected in a resolution of the White House Conference on Library and Information Science.

That same conference also resolved that the library is responsible for designing its services to meet the community's needs. The library's public relations efforts should shoulder part of this burden as well, by providing communication to the library about the public's needs.

This article concerns how three groups—library trustees, the public, and the library staff—can be involved in better communication between the community and the library. All three can exercise great creativity in promoting the public library. The trustees and the public are in a position both to inform the library about what the community needs and enjoys and to act with the library in presenting services to the community, especially visible and attractive programs. Perhaps librarians can cultivate enthusiasm and active cooperation between itself and the other two groups, as well as fully utilizing the enthusiasm of its own staff. Although this article does not attempt to present a procedural model for the public library's program of public relations, it does give a number of lesser procedures that gather information for the library about what is attractive to the community and how to organize and present services, particularly programs and exhibits, that will elicit public attention.

THE BOARD OF TRUSTEES

The library's board of trustees is in a cardinal position in the public relations program. On one hand, members represent the community to the library and govern the library on behalf of the community. On the other hand, they represent the library to the community, particularly to the municipal officials, and, by establishing the library's policies, determine how the library is to meet the community's needs. The policy for public relations is among the policies for which the library board is ultimately responsible.

The library board acts on behalf of the community. Its perceptions are those of lay participants who can seek, even demand library services from the position of those who need them. If the board is constituted of representatives of a diversity of groups and interests in the community, so much the better. But even if it is not, the board is a group dedicated to library services and intellectual freedom from the perspective of the user of those services. As Virginia Young says, "It cannot be too firmly emphasized that the library board represents overall citizen control of the library. . . ."[1]

The board acts on behalf of the library in the community, too. The relationship of the library to local government, in particular, is in the hands of the library board. When setting its budget, the library board must be capable of informing the city council or other municipal authority of the amount and quality of library service that has been delivered in the past and how the needs have been assessed at which new or modified library programs are aimed. The board should have on hand the list of accomplishments of the library and some statistics—how many people used the library, how many attended special programs, and how many the library has failed to reach. The librarian informs the city council through the board and must equip the board with relevant information. Although the board's interaction with the government is crucial at the time of setting the budget, the interaction should continue throughout the year, to keep some attention on the activities of the library. Quarterly reports are a good idea.

The board of trustees also presents the library to the community through the library itself; that is, the board is ultimately responsible for library services and the promotion of those services. For this reason, the board should formally adopt a public relations policy. The following model policy statement is designed for public libraries and can be adapted to local situations.

Public Relations Policy Statement

In recognition of the _____ Library's responsibility to maintain continuing communication with present and potential users of the library's services and resources so as to assure effective and maximum usage by all citizens, the Board of Trustees of the _____ Library adopts the following resolution as a matter of policy.

The objectives of the library's public relations program are:
To promote community awareness of library services;
To stimulate public interest in and usage of the library;
To develop public understanding and support of the library and its role in the community.

The following means may be used to accomplish these objectives:

1. The library director or a designated qualified staff member shall have the responsibility for coordinating the public relations and public information activities.

2. Surveys of the community shall be made as needed to assure the _____ Library's responsiveness to the interests and needs of all citizens.

3. Personal and informational group contacts shall be maintained with government officials, opinion leaders, service clubs, civic associations, and other community organizations by library staff and board members.

4. Training sessions, workshops, and other aids shall be made available to library staff members to assure courteous, efficient, and friendly contact with library patrons and the general public.

5. An annual plan of specific goals and activities shall be developed, sufficient funds shall be allocated to carry out the program, and the program shall be evaluated periodically.

6. The _____ Library may sponsor programs, classes, exhibits, and other library-centered activities and shall cooperate with other groups in organizing these to fulfill the community's needs for educational, cultural, informational, or recreational opportunities.

7. Local media shall be utilized to keep the public aware of and informed about the _____ Library's resources and services.

8. Newsletters, brochures, and other promotional materials shall be produced and distributed through regular mailings and other effective methods of reaching the public.

Beyond adopting a general policy, the board will be responsible for confirming or modifying the actual plans for P.R. activities or programs, which are developed in detail and executed by the library staff. The trustees can individually be creative in making suggestions for activities, learning from their contacts with the community and other community leaders, and taking inspiration from P.R. efforts of other organizations they know.

THE PUBLIC

The public is the target of the public relations effort. While not ordinarily involved in the actual planning of the program (except for the Friends of the Library organization, which is often heavily involved in public relations), the public is the group whose needs must be discovered, to whom service is directed, and who must be alerted to the resources of the library.

Both finding out and shaping how the public views the library are goals of the P.R. program. The public library has certain advantages in which its tradition of service and its public image meet. Public libraries have long been more than well-equipped study halls. They have held exhibits, been places for performances, and provided facilities for meetings since the early twentieth century. Lectures and exhibits concerned not only books but also paintings, rugs, porcelains, and other objects of art; libraries housed industrial and commercial displays. Even the ubiquitous Carnegie-funded library was "more than a place for the storage and dissemination of books. It was also a general community center in which art exhibitions, lecture and recital rooms, organs, and even gymnasiums, bowling alleys, and swimming pools would sometimes be available."[2]

The public library is, in fact, ideally suited to meet cultural needs because its resources are interrelated. Concerts, for example, are reinforced by and reinforce the use of biographies of composers, recordings, musical histories, and sheet music. Cooking demonstrations encourage participants to use a cookbook to try their own hands and to read about the countries of origin of different cuisines. Art exhibits open whole ranges of art history books, biographies of artists, slides, and pictures to the use of their viewers. The diversity has another advantage, too, in providing an opportunity to people who prefer to learn by one method rather than another.

Learning More from the Public in the Library

Learning about the library's clientele in the library can produce a great deal of information about those the library is trying to serve. For a very small library, learning about library users may involve simply asking the person with a reference question, "For what sort of project do you need this information?" which is often part of the reference interview anyway. The point is to keep in mind the more interesting and frequent projects. In a larger library, a box should be available into which all staff members can put notes about the more striking projects of library users; the notes can mention ideas for programs on the basis of users' projects.

A Little Survey

Contacting already established local organizations is another way of learning about your community, its needs, and the sorts of programs that would attract people. The library can survey the members of these organizations to learn about their lifestyles, interests, and information needs. The library should list all of the organizations in town and call their presidents, asking for a place in their programs some time within the next two or three months. If their programs have been set, the librarian can ask for a few minutes in the business agenda.

The library should write or adapt a simple survey form that the librarian can take to the meetings, distribute, and use to explain why the library is interested in the organization. Read the questions on the survey, asking people to answer them as they are read. It is important to collect the completed forms at the meeting. If any time is left, the librarian can talk about the library services and respond to questions.

This survey makes a contact between the library and many people who, perhaps, do not use the library. It provides information on the basis of which to plan programs of library service. If the library publicizes the plan for the survey and, later, its results, it will inform the whole community of the library's interest.

Other advantages of the organization-based survey can be found. One is that the library can ask each organization to appoint a liaison to the library: these liaisons form the nucleus of a Friends of the Library group. The librarian can also, in developing friendly relations with the group, request contributions for things the library needs—a new movie projector, for example, an expensive reference work, or even contributions of labor, such as for remodeling. The greatest value lies in the organization's involvement in the library.

The Full Survey

Neither of the preceding ideas substitutes adequately for a full and statistically valid survey of the community. This is not the place to offer guidelines for preparing such a survey, selecting a sample for it, or carrying it out. *A Planning Process for Public Libraries* (ALA, 1980) contains a description of the survey process, contents of a survey form, and references for further reading on conducting and interpreting surveys. It shows how to coordinate the survey with other information about the community and how to incorporate information about the community in a broader planning process.

The full survey is, however, expensive and time consuming, even if some of the work is done by volunteers. The P.R. program must take advantage of other sources of community information, rather than wait for the completion of a postponed, elaborate survey.

USING THE PUBLIC IN PUBLIC RELATIONS

Informal questioning of people in the library can lead not only to topics, but also to people who can offer programs in the library. So can reading newspapers, even advertisements. The names of local experts appear in many places, sometimes accidentally—a person asking a question about one thing may know quite a lot about something else and might be asked, later, to offer a program. Ideas for programs and exhibits are usually the result of a staff member seeing or hearing something that clicks as a useful library idea. The trick is how to foster this "clicking" in *all* staff, and to ensure that the seminal ideas are passed on to a person with power to bring them to fruition. All kinds of things are ready and available. Examples of what the library might run into are weaving goat hair (known to have happened), making cheese (worth a shot through a nature store, extension service, or out-and-out experiment by the staff), locating some rag books (if impossible, it doesn't matter) and the gathering of toys and games (patrons and stores should make that a breeze). Quick and easy brainstorming can yield a wealth of information, a rich diversity of programs, and the involvement of staff and patrons. Certainly, programs can be organized "the other way around." One could decide reasonable topics and then seek speakers by their specialty. But that approach takes time, lots of it, and, in the end, it may not yield the hoped-for result. More important, it may not involve the people who already have a "feel" for the library—its philosophy, its value—and who wish to add their gifts to the endeavor. Assuming that the telephone and desk communications in a library are positive, there will be patron resources available. Staff should be thinking of these possibilities in their daily contacts. Whether the connections are made at the moment of discovery ("Do you have a moment? I know our children's librarian would love to talk to you about cheesemaking!") or conveyed indirectly at a later time, the important thing is to pass the idea on!

Contacts with community organizations can be particularly profitable in planning programs. The library can invite key members of the community, media, subject experts, etc., to serve on an honorary or advisory committee. The honorary committee can provide support, status, and recognition. The advisory committee can share expertise by offering suggestions regarding program content, promotion, funding, etc. Members should be chosen carefully and should understand that they are advisory. Both of these groups can be promoters as they talk with their associates about their involvement with the library.

Planning an event in conjunction with another organization is possible, too. By doing this, the library has direct access to a whole new group of users. The other organization doubles the impact of the program through its own press releases, through its members being available for interviews, and by providing a new network for poster or brochure distribution. For a series on interior design, the library might work with a local design group. This group could provide materials for an exhibit, contribute to a lecture series, and provide funding. This works because it is to their interest as well as yours to promote the event.

The Friends group is another organization that can help plan, promote, sponsor, and pay for an event. In turn, it is important to do something special for them, too. You may perhaps offer a private screening, lecture, reception, or opening just for them.

THE LIBRARY STAFF: PLANNING, PROGRAMMING, PACKAGING, AND PUBLICITY

Good library service is the best way for the library to relate to the public. For this reason, the attitude of the staff is fundamental to the library's P.R. program. The staff must be encouraged and reminded that their work is important, and they should be treated with the respect they deserve from library management. The chapter of this book on staff relations provides some ways to ensure good communication within the library.

The library staff is also the place where most of the creativity in the library's program of public relations will be found. In all aspects of service, the staff learns from library users and, if it knows the library management to be open-minded, will pass the suggestions and requests for better service, programs, and better ways to present services, to those administrators with the authority to bring such things about.

Library workers are often compulsive readers. Traveling, dining out, in offices, at festivals and fairs, they cannot resist grabbing papers of all kinds. If they should discover a flyer of special merit that deserves wide community exposure, an effort can be made by the library to get multiples. These can be distributed at programs or exhibits. The more eyes scouting, the better.

The person in charge of the suggestion box has a marvelous source of ideas. There might be direct program suggestions. Then too, when requests pile up for books on a given topic, it indicates a community interest that might warrant some program or exhibit attention. Questions posed at the reference desk likewise suggest program possibilities. Sudden bursts of interest in a topic should be probed. A few discussions with the patrons bringing in requests will often produce not only a topic, but some leads on local experts. Newspapers and telephone books bring "out of the blue" ideas to staff members as well. In pursuit of a rabies shot, someone might discover a nifty new veterinarian who owns a pair of Peruvian chinchillas!

Brainstorming sessions, which should be brief, can suggest ways to package or present these materials. Suppose you have an idea for a summer series for children on *America: Past and Present* to complement the historical society's July 4 festivities, and a suggestion box containing the following:

> P. Jones has horses, goats, cows. Willing to bring. 555–0009
> Computer game exhibit? Electronic company willing to help.
> Tutors needed for adults.
> Kay Fendwick makes own butter in churn. Story hour? 555–6666

Curbside jump rope rhymes. Under sprinkler? New book in!
Nancy Teprup is back from a trip retracing Lewis & Clark—
excellent slides. 555–5217
More catalog drawers. Please!?
Grace Thompson plays mumblety peg and has lots of old toys.
Loves to share, do programs. 555–0122

Five minutes of brainstorming might provide the rudiments of a full program:

Past. Life on a farm: horses (shoeing, riding, caring for)
                    cows (milking, butter making)
                    goats (weaving, milk, cheese)
   Games: Festival of good old time fun with bladder balloons, mud ball, mumblety-peg, sawdust dolls
   Stories: Readings from rag books
Present. Computer exhibit
   Slides: Wilderness tour retracing Lewis and Clark expeditions today
   Games: Festival of the latest toys and games
   Stories: Readings from staff favorites, locally written/unpublished manuscripts.

Every member of the library staff has ideas, talents, and interests that can form the basis of a program. Every one owns something that could be an item to exhibit. A moment spent with other library staff (friends and Board as well) in the course of the process called the Freelance Programming Mini-Workshop that follows can produce ideas for programs. Such a mini-workshop is designed to draw out personal potential and apply it to programs for the community.

FREELANCE PROGRAMMING MINI-WORKSHOPS

1. Write down a program contribution you could offer. Think about these ideas:
   What games do you play? Baseball, football, street hockey, Scrabble, penny pitch, Candyland, jump rope. Wouldn't you be able to handle a town checker fest? A jump-rope marathon? A staff/community baseball game?
   What do you like to cook? Wouldn't you be able to generate: Halloween apple day? A gigantic mess o' greens? A spice advice table? A natural nibble day?

What hobbies do you have? Hiking, sewing, carpentry, refinishing, ballet, weightlifting. How about a short stroll in a park for moms and preschoolers? A birdhouse hanging hike? A miniworkout with three-pound weights?

Do you have travel slides? Could you arrange them for a story hour? An elementary school visit? A lunch break?

Personal Program Contribution: _____

2. Write down an exhibit contribution you could make. Think about the following sort of things:

What old things do you have? Quilts, car ornaments, adding machines, farm tools, doorknobs, dolls.

What do you collect? Family pictures, posters, arrowheads, geodes, angel ornaments, local history memorabilia.

What equipment do you have to support your favorite sports? Rubber boats, kayaks, skis, bikes, racquets, helmets.

What apparatus or implements or paraphernalia do your friends, neighbors, spouses use at work? Microscope, banjo, rock tumbler, magnifying glass, easel, litmus paper, drain pipes, galvanometers. Couldn't you snare a friend for an exhibit demo, or story hour?

Personal exhibit contribution: _____

3. Now that those are recorded, scan your latest local newspaper(s) for an upcoming event that might attract an audience of interest to the library. You do not need or want to be a cosponsor. For this exercise, you are looking for an event at which the library might cooperate without having to do the basic organizational, promotional work.

Event to attend: _____

4. What sort of participation/enrichment can the library offer to this event? Share your group members' program and exhibit capabilities. Enjoy this! Take time to discover the person you thought you worked with every day.

Review library programs/services you might wish to advertise.

Library's contribution: _____

5. Consider ways to attract attention.
   Come up with your "pitch line."
   Determine your focal point. Is it to be demonstration?
   A display? A particular person?
   Will you be handing out printed materials? If so, on what
   subject?
   Attraction getters: _____

6. What materials will you need to complet the project? a
   table? volunteers? costumes? posters?
   Materials: _____

Plan for this workshop to take 30 minutes. It should yield many
workable ideas for future programs.

Several more examples of how to package the ideas that
might come from the mini workshop, contacts with library
users, cooperation with other organizations, and brainstorming
will be useful.

A series on Shakespeare could include an exhibit on the Globe
Theatre, Elizabethan England, or special editions of Shakespeare's works. A film series with such features as *Romeo and
Juliet* (Hussey), *Taming of the Shrew* (Burton and Taylor), *King
Lear* (Scofield), *Richard III* (Olivier) could complement this
exhibit. A less traditional series might include film adaptations
of Shakespeare's works with *West Side Story* (*Romeo and Juliet*),
Double Life (*Othello*) and *Throne of Blood* (*MacBeth*). Recordings
of live plays of Shakespeare from the library's collection also
could be highlighted.

The following is another example of an integrated series that
is most promotable. A "Salute to Fashion Series" could be made
up of the following components: fashion shows (designer's,
manufacturer's, contest winners or store previews); a fashion
artisans' fair with weaving, fabric painting, leatherwork,
beaded jewelry, garment construction; panel discussions including careers in fashion or fashion photography; fashion films
such as *Sweet Charity* with costumes designed by Edith Head
and *The Women* with costumes designed by Adrian; "meet the
designers" programs; a fashion workshop with sessions on cos-
metics, the working wardrobe, and fashions to make one feel
younger. A bibliography which would coordinate the library's

resources could include sections on such aspects of fashion as: designing, construction, wearing, its makers and their creations, its historical tradition, marketing.

Another method of packaging is to use a flyer, brochure, or bookmark. A brochure on the 1940s might include a listing of such current programs as concerts of 40s tunes, lectures on the life and times, a selection of 40s films, an exhibit of photographs from the era. A bookmark with the 1940s as the topic could include histories, biographies, recordings, etc.

A bibliography for a series can become a source of enjoyment and information in itself. Such a bibliography might deal with the Christmas holiday season and be called "It's a Tradition." Sections might include holiday customs and traditions (with a quote regarding a custom before the actual materials listing), recipes (with a sample recipe for wassail), decorating and gift ideas (with directions for making a Ceppo, an Italian Christmas tree), a section on holidays in literature (perhaps with Mark Twain's Christmas wish), then carols, classics and pops (with brief lyrics such as those from "Bring a Torch, Jeannette, Isabella"). On this bibliography/resource guide, it would be helpful to have a reference to the events planned with times and locations noted. It's also good to mention that the materials listed in the brochure/bibliography are only a fraction of the many books, etc., available in the library.

One part of packaging is the need to find a phrase that helps promote the idea the best. The following are some which might be used with an "International Festival: Up, Up, and Away" (travel); "Point of View" (foreign films); "All the World's a Stage" (international performances); "Children's World" (children's program); "Everybody Dance" (dance series); "Spice of Life" (cooking demonstrations); "A Literary Spectrum" (discussions on literature). To help find that phrase to complete the package, brainstorm with your staff. For brainstorming it's imperative to provide an accepting attitude, so that the best ideas can emerge, even if they seem silly at first.

Finally, the kinds of promotion suitable for a public library should be mentioned. *Direct mail* (print and distribute a monthly calendar of events, send letters to schools and community groups); *paid advertisements* (in the daily newspapers, as well as weekly community papers); *public service announcements* (PSAs) (fifteen-, thirty-, and sixty-second announcements for the radio and television); *printed materials* (flyers with the "five w's": who, what, where, when, why); *visual materials* (banners on street poles and on the side of your library, signs in parades and car cards in buses); *interviews* (the library should seek out radio and television stations to tell your story, and a staff member prepare facts, interesting stories, and what the library wants to get across ahead of time); *word of mouth* (the library should involve key community leaders in planning events and in talking to community groups); as well as *press releases, photo alerts*, and *press kits*. When introducing one program, be sure to mention the others that are coming up. How to go about some of these tasks will be discussed later in this book.

A reception should accompany the opening of an important exhibit. Those who cooperated in preparing the exhibit—library staff, trustees, and the press—can be invited. Invitations to local politicians will keep the library in their eyes, even if few come to the reception itself. (A good rate of return for such an invitation is thirty percent.)

Promoting your library should be a way of life. An example of this occurred recently when one of us sat next to our director of public information of the Chicago Public Library at a book and author luncheon in a local hotel. In her hand she had a bundle of folders she planned to place in a conspicuous place. The P.R. expert knew that this audience was a potential audience for the library's events, cared enough about the institution to think of its promotion at every opportunity, and was aggressive enough to follow through.

Getting the public involved in the library requires the interaction of the library with politicians, community leaders, other organizations in the community, local business, and other local interests. It also demands careful attention to the people who actually come to the library and to the reasons why they come. The creativity of all these groups, combined with that of the library staff, can bring about activities that encourage commitment on all parts to the library and its role.

NOTES

1. Virginia G. Young, *Trustee of a Small Public Library* (Chicago: American Library Ass., 1978).
2. Rosemary Du Mont, *Reform and Reaction* (Westport, Conn.: Greenwood Pr., 1977), p. 63.

Jon Eldredge

Internal Public Relations for the Academic Library

Public relations has become a topic of great interest to academic librarians, and with good reason. Serious declines in student enrollment and decreasing budgets have forced many institutions of higher education in the United States to critically evaluate expenditures made in all areas of their programs. Academic libraries are not exempt from these considerations nor can they afford to be. While librarians are certainly aware of the importance of library services to the health of academic institutions, they too often fail to communicate this idea effectively to those who use the library. When carefully developed and administered, a public relations program provides the best possible means of communicating the library's mission to the academic community.

Few articles of significance on the subject of public relations for academic libraries have appeared in the library literature since the early 1960s. As a result of the recent flurry of excitement among librarians[1] we can expect more to be written on the subject during the next few years. In contrast, there are many publications directed toward public libraries on the topic of public relations, but because academic libraries serve the needs of an entirely different clientele, they can borrow only a few techniques from public libraries. Academic libraries need to design P.R. programs appropriate to the special interests of their users.

Academic libraries normally operate within a fragile network of relationships that permeate their campus communities. In such closed systems, libraries must carefully plan and implement all of their P.R. activities.

PUBLIC RELATIONS IN THE ACADEMIC LIBRARY

Public relations is an institution's or organization's ongoing effort to communicate reliable information about itself to particular groups and individuals and to receive information from them. In academic librarianship, this means a program planned to heighten awareness among a specific group of people about the range of available library materials and services. It also means promoting library resources and services by presenting them in a favorable light.

Initiating a P.R. program can never be an immediate remedy for a problem incurred by a library that has alienated the community it serves; a good P.R. program promises no quick solution, nor can it gloss over poor service.[2] Instead, public relations can more precisely be interpreted to mean the "planned, deliberate and sustained effort to establish and maintain mutual understanding between an organization (the library) and its public."[3] In essence, public relations means a healthy communication between the library and the public.

A P.R. program for an academic library normally consists of three components: the political, the external, and the internal. The political component involves the process of securing economic support for the library from potential funding sources. These sources are usually limited to the college or university administration. They may also include sources of support from the private and public sectors.

External public relations seeks to communicate accurate information about the library's services and materials to persons outside the walls of the library. In so doing, external P.R. efforts hope to fully encourage use of the library's resources. Course-related library instruction would be considered part of a library's external P.R. effort.

Finally, internal public relations involves the methods an academic library may use within its building or buildings to inform users about the range of services and materials the library provides. Internal P.R. efforts also seek to encourage interested library users to utilize these resources.

The academic library's total P.R. program is thus a complex scheme. To maintain healthy relations with groups both inside and outside the library requires an enormous amount of persistence, tact, time, and energy. Because of the complexity of explaining the entire spectrum of P.R. activities an academic library may normally undertake, this essay will focus instead on describing only the internal component of a P.R. program for a college or university library. Although the political and external components of public relations vary greatly from library to library, P.R. activities inside the academic library have a remarkably consistent and structured form. The common contents of the internal P.R. program—signage, publications, orientation programs, and exhibits—are common-sense, proven aids to communicating with library users. The fundamental internal P.R. effort—good service—is partly fostered by staff relations, which are discussed elsewhere in this volume.

RESPONSIBILITY

The library director usually attends to the external and political areas of public relations for the library. Internal P.R. becomes the responsibility of a subordinate, preferably someone immediately below the director in the organizational hierarchy, and, often, the head of public service. The size of the professional library staff will ultimately determine who will take on this responsibility. Ideally, there should be a P.R. department with at least one full-time public information officer. Although Although in a large university library the associate director may be assigned this task, in a college library the reference librarian may find himself or herself in charge.

Such a person should possess certain qualifications. He or she should be trained in the skills of public relations and should be knowledgeable about, and adept at, communications and publicity techniques. Aside from a friendly and sincere manner, he or she should be sensitive to the needs of library users and staff, even if these needs are never articulated. The public relations officer should "show initiative and resourcefulness, and be blessed with much tact. Above all, such a person should manifest a contagious enthusiasm."[4]

Every librarian and staff member who works with the public, from the reference librarian to the circulation desk clerk, should participate in the internal P.R. program. To insure a well-coordinated and consistent program, though, the person designated by the director as responsible for internal public relations should have the authority to coordinate all such activities.[5]

The librarian managing internal public relations must be certain the goals of the program reflect those goals set forth by the library. In most instances the library will have an official statement of purpose or mission. The librarian in charge of internal public relations should review this document carefully. If the library has, in addition, any unstated but still strongly maintained goals, the librarian should learn them and their implications as soon as possible from the director and other professionals on the staff. The same formula applies if the library has no stated goals. It is pointless to promote an enigma, so the goals must be discovered at the beginning of the public relations program.

The librarian responsible for internal public relations will want to draw a clear distinction between short-term and long-term goals for the library. An appropriate example of a short-term goal would be the activity known as "publicity." The terms "publicity" and "public relations," though often used interchangeably in casual conversation, should never be confused. Publicity is the activity employed by a library to draw the attention of the public to its services and programs. Public relations, in contrast, addresses the issue of quality of the relationship between the library and its public.

How does the librarian in charge of public relations interpret library goals? How does this librarian integrate library goals into the P.R. program? An example involving a small academic library might illustrate the process of interpretation. Imagine such a small academic library, one possessing a good but limited collection. Such a library will need to pursue the goal of supplementing its on-site resources with an interlibrary loan service. The P.R. program should be planned to communicate reliable information about interlibrary loan to potential users of the service. In addition, the program should turn user attention away from the small size of the collection, and focus it instead upon the vast possibilities of access offered by the interlibrary loan service. Under these circumstances, the P.R. program could present the library to its users as being the *link* between themselves and the world of recorded knowledge. Both the existing collection and the interlibrary loan service will receive a positive image by utilizing this theme. The theme of linkage can be woven into a variety of internal and external P.R. activities. At faculty meetings, at library orientation, and in library instruction sessions, librarians can portray the library as the necessary link between the audience and their success in an area highly dependent upon recorded information and ideas. Library publications such as brochures, student handbooks, and perhaps even bookmarks might also convey the image of linkage for the library. In public service activities, reference librarians can communicate the idea of interlibrary loan as a supplement to on-site library materials by encouraging use of the interlibrary loan service.

Large and small academic libraries alike might pursue the goal of providing library instruction for all students. The P.R. program could, in this example, interpret this goal by communicating the idea of students becoming self-reliant library users. The P.R. program could present this theme through the various communication channels such as the ones described in the previous example. Library orientation for incoming students would be a particularly good time to communicate this theme of self-reliance in using the library. It should be noted that the process of interpreting library goals must take into account the personalities of library staff members involved in the P.R. program, which very possibly will include everyone on the staff. The administrative philosophy of the library also will have a strong influence upon the interpretation of goals and the evolution of a P.R. program.

Goals for the library will vary from institution to institution. Every academic library serves a unique group of users, and goals for the library must address the needs of these users. In general, however, the long-term goals for an academic library can usually be summarized as follows:

> To support the curriculum of the college or university by making available relevant library materials and services.
> To provide the institution's researchers with needed library materials through both regular collection development and participation in an interlibrary loan network.[6]

Of course, other goals, such as the education of students on the most effective use of the library (library instruction), may be added to this list, depending upon the mission of the library.

The remainder of this paper will point out some principles for use of the most common elements of the public relations program in the academic library: signage, orientation programs, library publications, and exhibits.

SIGNAGE

Step inside a shopping center anywhere in the United States and you will witness a remarkable phenomenon: consumers, faced with an almost overwhelming array of stores and products in the shopping center, are usually able to locate quickly what they need. Even a newcomer to such a complex of stores can be guided to a desired destination by utilizing the system of well-thought out floor diagrams and store directories provided. Supermarkets, too, employ a similar system of signs in every aisle to direct shoppers to products. An increasing number of nonprofit institutions such as museums have begun to recognize the practical aspects of improved signs and floor diagrams. Directional aids also fulfill a more subtle promotional purpose. In the process of directing people to whatever they are looking for, these aids can also heighten public awareness of other available goods and services.

To a certain extent, the principles that apply to directional aids in the commercial world are applicable to academic libraries. At the same time, though, it seems dangerously simplistic to equate libraries with department stores and supermarkets. Academic libraries house materials and offer services that are certainly far more complex than those normally found in the consumer world.

A P.R. program seeks to make first impressions of the academic library positive ones so users will want to examine library resources more closely. How often, though, does an academic library's staff and administration take the time to ponder what other people see as they enter and attempt to use the library? How often does the new student or a first-time visitor to the library perceive the overall plan of the building by viewing either clearly printed directional signs or floor diagrams? "In the library, or any other institution for that matter," observes Mona Garvey, "no prior knowledge should be assumed."[7] If academic library public relations advances the goal of making its resources available to the academic community, then it first has to indicate *where* the user can find needed services and materials. And, if a college or university library makes the effort to do this, it suggests to the user that the library wants to be of service—and this person will truly feel more inclined to seek out the additional resources he or she needs. Many institutions and businesses are now designed for self-service,[8] and if the library provides familiar kinds of directional aids, the user will feel more at ease and will be more inclined to further utilize library services and materials.

Directional aids, important as they are, should be used only when necessary, however.[9] Otherwise the library will assume a cluttered appearance. In the entrance lobby, for example, these aids should simply point the way toward major services such as information desks, circulation counters, computer terminals, reference departments, and the catalog. Floor plans, building directories, and directional signs should be strategically located to catch one's immediate attention.

Mona Garvey offers the following insights: "Signs should be carefully worded to give information without offense. It is always best to stress the positive rather than the negative."[10] To understand the latter point better, simply compare the difference between the sound and wording of the phrases "No Smoking" and "Thank you for not smoking."

An artist should be commissioned to design and compose diagrams that are attractive and easily understood. Some institutions of higher education have sufficient on-campus resources to produce library signage and directional aids, greatly reducing the cost of such a project. Librarians who plan to develop directional aids for their libraries should probably visit other libraries first to learn from the mistakes as well as the successes of other institutions. They should consider which services and materials are most often sought. They may wish to hire a consultant, probably an architect, to get advice on color coordination, sign shape, lettering size and other considerations. Recently Dorothy Pollett and Peter Haskell published a timely book on library signage. Entitled *Sign Systems for Libraries*, it is a useful guide in developing practical and attractive directional aids.[11] Another useful guide is *A Sign System for Libraries* by Mary S. Mallery and Ralph E. DeVore, published by ALA.

ORIENTATION PROGRAMS

Orientation can be the ideal opportunity to present the academic library in a favorable light to new and impressionable students. Incoming students usually know little about the services and layout of the library. For the most part, they perceive it to be a place where they will spend much of their time while earning a degree. Before entering college, many freshmen probably used their high school or public libraries largely as study halls. They view the academic library with indifference or perhaps even with a slightly negative attitude. If presented in the appropriate manner, however, library orientation can create fresh, more positive attitudes toward the library for these students. Because it can produce widespread and favorable first impressions of the library, a P.R. program should include orientation activities for new students. Unfortunately, academic libraries traditionally have neglected the orientation process. In spite of the potential benefits to be gained by presenting successful orientation programs, such ventures are normally viewed as a low priority item by academic libraries. Thus, insufficient personnel and financial resources are allocated toward developing worthwhile orientation programs. The paradox of this whole matter is that most librarians seem to think students, particularly the new ones, need an in-depth orientation to the library.[12]

Why, then, do librarians neglect the orientation process if it offers an opportunity to positively shape student attitudes toward the academic library? For one thing, librarians simply are unaware of just how great an impact orientation can have on the attitudes of students. Librarians also are generally unaware of what freshmen experience during their first shaky days at college; or they have forgotten just how hectic this period was in their own academic lives. To overcome this barrier, librarians responsible for library orientation might want to consult the dean of students to understand better the psyches of new students as they adjust to campus life. It is also wise for librarians to join or observe the meetings of the campus-wide orientation committee to view the process of orientation in a broader perspective. Moreover, colleagues who serve on such committees may be able to offer useful suggestions to librarians on the design and implementation of an orientation program for the library.

Finally, it seems orientation has been neglected due to the lingering confusion of library orientation with the more complex activity called library instruction. It appears that since both library instruction and orientation evolved out of the same concern, that of familiarizing students with library resources, the two activities have continued to be equated with one another. In their present forms, however, the two activities pursue distinctly different goals. Library instruction seeks to teach students *how* to most effectively utilize library resources for research. Library orientation, in contrast, simply introduces the concept of an academic library to new students and familiarizes them with the physical layout of the building. The two activities, orientation and instruction, thus obviously pursue different goals; yet apparently many librarians apply professional expectations to orientation really applicable only to library instruction. Consequently, when students later demonstrate a low retention of the information they received during orientation, librarians evaluating the cognitive outcomes of the orientation have incorrectly concluded the program was a failure.

At this time, library orientation still seems to be a crude art in need of further development, possibly due to a lack of recognition of its importance and due, in part, to confusion about its purpose. Nevertheless, there are some fairly useful methods currently employed that offer some guidance as to how library orientation might be conducted.

Guided Tours

Orientation tours are intended primarily to familiarize students with the plan of the library. Large groups can be led around the library, which will allow the librarian to speak in a loud enough voice for everyone to hear. When the building is in use, smaller groups are necessary to avoid disturbing library users. Tours offer the advantage of presenting the librarians as helpful, pleasant human beings to students. However, given the format, services can be only superficially described.

Self-guided Tours

These typically appear in two formats, the taped cassette on a player with headphones and the printed booklet.[13] Such tours allow new students to proceed through the building at their own speed and level of interest. When students become interested in particular features before them, they can take time to stop and examine these features in more detail before proceeding at their leisure. Self-guided tours offer the additional advantage of causing no disturbance to persons studying and can be taken at the user's convenience. Unfortunately, students will rarely volunteer to involve themselves in such methods of orientation, since they often have little motivation to learn about the library at the beginning of the school year.

Video Programs

These programs can be presented in the library or the classroom at a mutually agreed upon time. The author has viewed several of these programs and has found them to be both entertaining and useful. The high cost, due to the length of production time and the amount of personnel resources involved, does pose an obstacle to implementing this kind of orientation program. However, universities with large numbers of undergraduate students and limited staff resources to allocate to orientation tours may want to consider carefully the advantages of this form of orientation.

Slide-tape Programs

When a script has been carefully written for recording on a sound track, and the slides photographed with skill, these programs can create a very professional image for the library. Many librarians have grossly underestimated the amount of time necessary to produce worthwhile slide-tape programs and later have been dissatisfied with the results, as have the audiences. Yet, these programs offer the same advantages as video programs without the high cost of purchasing video equipment and hiring personnel to produce these video shows.

Receptions

Normally these functions are reserved for the orientation of faculty members new to the college or university libraries. Libraries generally try to discourage the consumption of food and drink in their buildings and so, during new student orientation, they tend to shy away from sponsoring a reception, as this might give a misleading impression of regular routines and operations. In contrast, Venable Lawson has strongly advocated the use of receptions for new student orientation as a means to radically alter the freshmen's conceptions of academic libraries and librarians.[14]

To be sure, the several approaches to library orientation do achieve some measure of success when properly planned. In the coming years, other approaches will likely develop. As of now, no safe formula can dictate how to plan and conduct the ideal orientation program. Perhaps the most relevant guidelines to apply to the process are for the library to concentrate on favorably introducing to new students its purpose, services, personnel, and physical arrangement. In presenting orientation programs a library should impart only that amount of information new students will absolutely need to know during their initial exposure to an academic library.

LIBRARY PUBLICATIONS

The printed materials an academic library produces are a sensitive matter and should be approached with deliberation and care. Because the library still has as its chief service the provision of the printed word, and since there appears to be an abundance of paper filling up the lives of most persons in the academic world, the library's publications should be distinctive. They should stand out from competing printed materials if not in the quality of substances used, then at least by the amount of thought put into communicating ideas and information to users. An academic library can produce various forms of printed materials. The most common of these are library handbooks, guides to special collections or services, periodic newsletters reporting news about the library and, of course, bibliographies. A number also publish union catalogs of serials. Some libraries distribute bookmarks, accessions lists, and current awareness bulletins.

Library publications should be carefully worded and provide only enough material to communicate the desired message. With budget restrictions it can be easily understood why a library would wish to spend less on certain publications than on others. It should be remembered, however, that "poorly produced library publications will not only fail to make an impact but will also help to reinforce a poor image of the library."[15] High standards of quality should be maintained. Therefore it has been suggested that "each publication should be produced in a manner and by methods consistent with its purpose."[16] A library handbook should have more time and energy devoted to its composition and layout, for example, than an accessions list of new fiction titles, since the handbook will have a longer lasting and more profound impact upon the user.

In general it is best to consciously choose a format for all library publications that can be recognized at a glance. Several methods might help achieve this goal. For one, a library's publications can set themselves apart by use of special paper; paper with a unique texture or color tone. Another approach may be to place a colored border on one or more sides of all sheets of printed matter. Once a specific color is chosen, it should be adhered to so that the color becomes associated with the library. In several British universities, this method of color-coding all library publications has proven to be quite successful. But the most successful and adaptable method for easy identification of library printed materials this author has observed is the use of visual library logos. Logos pictorially symbolize an institution, and, as a form of identification, are quite popular. Three effective library logos are those employed by the Harlan Hatcher Graduate Library at the University of Michigan, the Center for Research Libraries, and the University of York in England, shown in figures 1–3.

These logos are adaptable to a variety of library publications. They can be enlarged or reduced to conform to the physical size of the publication on which they appear. And they can be printed in a variety of colors, yet still be easily identified as part of a library's publications series.

Fig. 1. Logo developed for and used by the Harlan Hatcher Graduate Library, University of Michigan

LIBRARY MATERIALS
AVAILABLE FOR RESEARCH

from THE CENTER FOR
RESEARCH LIBRARIES

Fig. 2. Logo of the Center for Research Libraries. Reprinted by permission of the Center for Research Libraries.

Fig. 3. Logo of the University of York Library. Reprinted by permission of the University of York Library.

Library Guides

David Watkins has stated unequivocally that an academic library's most important publication is its library handbook.[17] Some college and university libraries prepare handbooks for faculty members,[18] but, in this discussion, student handbooks are the main concern. Library handbooks are designated to introduce the student to library resources relevant to his or her research and study needs. As a genre of library publication, handbooks are sometimes hard to characterize since their format and level of sophistication depend upon the particular academic library situation they are intended to introduce. Oyeniya Osundina of Nigeria, for instance, believes in the idea of a handbook, but favors breaking it up into one-page information sheets to serve as "aids and guide to every corner of the library."[19] In this plan, the card catalog, serials department, and other library services would make available brief, one-page statements of information about those services with enough "how-to-do-it" advice to familiarize the user with them and to get the user started on finding what he or she needs. Lake Forest College in Illinois utilizes a variation of Osundina's approach. Adjacent to the reference desk, users can find a rack of library guides. Each guide pertains to specific research problems: biography, periodical indexes, plagiarism, book reviews, and so on.

The prevalent opinion holds that library handbooks should consist of an actual book or pamphlet format. These handbooks are admittedly expensive to produce, but, if thoughtfully executed, they will make both an initial and lasting favorable impression on the student. They also will make the library more comprehensible and easier to use. Although handbooks vary from library to library, certain basic guidelines are suggested to assure a successful published introduction to the library. For one, the handbook should restrict itself to explaining services and features "just enough as is needed to use the library's basic services and . . . not too formally."[20] Instead of explaining in detail the many library services and regulations, the handbook should probably only refer the reader to the appropriate departments in situations that involve more complex explanations in order to maintain the reader's interest. One author has argued in favor of including light humor and illustration (such as floor diagrams, the parts of the cataloging card) within the text. Guy Lyle recommends that the handbook be designed to fit into a three-ring binder and that it also be distributed at new student orientation.[21]

Newsletters
At university libraries written communications usually appear in two forms. One informs the general university community about library news, the other circulates only among the staff. Sometimes these newsletters are combined into an all-purpose newsletter. Northwestern University circulates its staff newsletter in Chicago-area libraries and this combination appears to accomplish both internal and external P.R. objectives. The first kind of publication serves the users, telling them about recent events connected with the library, such as the acquisition of a rare book or the biographical sketch of a new librarian on the staff. Robert Orr has suggested that "the systematic release of library information on an informal basis at least once a month makes possible a timely and effective method of reporting."[22] It

also helps the public see the university research library as a human place rather than as a storage vault. Watkins feels the newsletter should also contain news from the publishing world and information about new and forthcoming books.[23] The internal newsletter serves a personnel function rather than a direct public relations function, by informing the staff about what is happening in the library. Yet, at the same time, a staff member who knows other staff and who receives regular information about the library's policies will most likely take more pride in his or her work.[24] The positive results will be conveyed as the staff member participates in public relations activities for the library.

Guides to Special Collections

Such publications vary in accordance with the collections they describe. As with the library handbooks, they should be easy to use and be located near the collections involved. They should also be placed near central lobbies and circulation desks to increase general awareness of these services among patrons.

Other Publications

Less common but effective in certain situations are the publishing of bibliographies, bookmarks, and accessions lists. Bibliographies may cover specialized academic disciplines or simply present a few pertinent books on current news event topics such as the conflict in the Middle East, the national energy conservation program, etc. Accessions lists might motivate people to check out new materials, but they also run the risk of getting tossed into the circular file since they are often lengthy and time-consuming to examine. Bookmarks distributed at check-out counters that list library hours, pertinent phone numbers for library departments and that announce monthly exhibits may also be a way to remind persons about library services in general.

EXHIBITS AND DISPLAYS

Displays and exhibits serve a dual function in the academic library. They call attention to special or relatively unknown resources offered by the library, and provide information, entertainment, and pleasure for library users. They can be an excellent device for enriching the library's P.R. program. Although often associated exclusively with the public library, exhibits and displays do have a place in the academic library. As Coplan has explained, "no library, regardless of its size, complexion or financial status, can afford to overlook exhibits as a means of widening its sphere of influence and service. . . ."[27] Mather has agreed and added that "worthwhile exhibits, intelligently presented and enthusiastically promoted, build up an amazing reservoir of good will" for the college or university library.[28]

Permanent exhibits are designed to serve long-term public relations program objectives. They can have an educational purpose, as in the case of the one located at Dartmouth College's Baker Library. In the main lobby of this library, students can view displays showing the steps involved in locating a book. Integrated into this permanent exhibit is a display tracing the history of the book. Every year, new students enter Dartmouth College and need to know this basic information, so the exhibit has a long-term status. In the face of a periodic turnover of its student population from term to term, Duke University's library has created a permanent photo exhibit of each member of the library staff to help students identify librarians. Thus, the students are able to recognize librarians when in need of library assistance. The exhibit also presents the library as an institution made up of people instead of a building where the university happens to store its books.[29] Temporary displays fulfill short-term P.R. objectives and so are kept in the library for about a month's duration. Temporary exhibits might involve the showing of anything from the presentation of a local artist's works to a display of new books on a topic of interest to the academic community. In general, temporary exhibits allow librarians to be more creative.

With exhibits and displays, an imaginative arrangement that integrates a theme, creative graphics, and color will attract attention. Eli Oboler thinks displays should be scheduled regularly and that topics selected for themes be calculated to be of wide public interest. He also points out "they take time—particularly planning time—and money."[30] Kate Coplan warns, too, that "amateurish, 'home-made' looking displays . . . should be avoided like the plague."[31] Nevertheless, for the purposes of improving internal library public relations, "Few library activities bring the rich rewards that displays do. If they are interesting enough and attractive enough and frequent enough, they can turn many indifferent viewers into active, enthusiastic library users and supporters."[32]

No single member of the library staff can be expected to dream up new and exciting ideas for an exhibit on a monthly basis. Every exhibit should be fresh and free of a narrow, routine perspective in order to hold the attention of regular library users. Therefore, all staff members, including student assistants, should be encouraged to participate in the creation and construction of the monthly exhibit. The person in charge of internal public relations at a university library can recruit individuals from its large staff to assume responsibility for each new exhibit. To evenly spread responsibility for setting up each monthly exhibit among all staff members, a university library will often establish a system of rotation. For example, in this scheme a staff member may assume the task of inventing and setting up a display only once every eighteen months. As a result, the rotation system leads to a series of exciting and different exhibit themes from month to month. To achieve a similar effect, the smaller academic library may occasionally want to invite faculty members or campus groups to design and implement the monthly exhibit. No matter who actually carries out the project, the person in charge of internal public relations should remain involved in this process from the beginning to the completion of the exhibit. In this capacity, he or she can act as a resource advisor as well as a friendly critic of proposed exhibit ideas.

CONCLUSION

The carefully planned internal P.R. program will yield positive results. To effect a better understanding between the library and its users, the program should include the activities described in this essay. Although each library will elect to utilize those activities in a manner appropriate to the needs of its users, the program must be carried out by a staff thoroughly committed to active public service. Only the presence of this healthy attitude will guarantee the success of all P.R. program activities for the academic library.

NOTES

1. The ALA Annual Meeting in New York during 1980 included several well-attended programs on the topic of public relations for academic libraries.

2. Denis Heathcote, "Public Relations and Publicity," in *Libraries in Higher Education: The User Approach to Service*, ed. John Cowley (London: Clive Bingley, 1975), p. 42.

3. R. G. Roberts, "Public Relations in Libraries," in *British Librarianship and Information Science 1966–1970* (London: Library Assn., 1972), p. 581.

4. Greta Renborg, "Public Relations Activities for the Stockholm City Library," *Scandinavian Public Library Quarterly* 3, no. 1: 13 (1970).

5. H. Vail Deale, "You Can Do It in College, Too," *Wilson Library Bulletin* 24: 514 (1950).

6. Steve Sherman, *ABC's of Library Promotion* (Metuchen, N.J.: Scarecrow, 1971), p. 158.

7. Mona Garvey, *Library Displays: Their Purpose, Construction and Use* (New York: Wilson, 1969), p. 17.

8. Ibid., p. 6.

9. Guy R. Lyle, *Administration of the College Library* (New York: Wilson, 1974), p. 273.

10. Garvey, p. 18.

11. Dorothy Pollett and Peter Haskell, *Sign Systems for Libraries: Solving the Wayfinding Problem* (New York: Bowker, 1979).

12. David W. Heron, "Public Relations of Academic Libraries," *College and Research Libraries* 16: 145 (1955).

13. Mary Jo Lynch, "Library Tours: The First Step," in *Educating the Library User*, ed. John Lubans (New York: Bowker, 1974), p. 259.

14. Venable Abram Lawson, "Assumptions of Academic Librarians—Builders of Barriers?" *Catholic Library World* 41: 236 (1969).

15. Heathcote, p. 45.

16. Ibid., p. 46.

17. David Roy Watkins, "Public Relations Possible through College Library Publications," *Catholic Library World* 19: 94 (1947).

18. Sr. Ann Bernard Goeddecke, "College Library Public Relations," *Catholic Library World* 46: 286 (1975).

19. Oyeniya Osundina, "The University Library in Nigeria and the Need for Public Relations," *Nigerian Libraries* 5, no. 2: 60 (1969).

20. Heathcote, p. 49.

21. Lyle, p. 269.

22. Robert. W. Orr, "Public Relations for College and University Libraries," *Library Trends* 1, no. 1: 128 (1952).

23. Watkins, p. 93.

24. L. A. Kenney, "Public Relations in the College Library," *College and Research Libraries* 25, no. 4: 264 (1969).

25. Harald Ostvold, "Public Relations in a University Library," *Missouri Library Association Quarterly* 10: 22 (1949).

26. Jane P. Kleiner, "The Information Desk: The Library's Gateway to Service," *College and Research Libraries* 29, no. 6: 501 (1968).

27. Kate Coplan, *Effective Library Exhibits* (Dobbs Ferry, N.Y.: Oceana, 1974), p. 1.

28. Lalit Mohan Mather, *Principles and Techniques of Educational Library Displays and Exhibits* (New Delhi: Mather, 1970), p. 4.

29. "Duke Exhibits Many Library Faces," *American Libraries* 8, no. 1: 15 (1977).

30. Eli M. Oboler, "Displays for the Academic Library," *Idaho Librarian* 22, no. 4: 138 (1970).

31. Coplan, p. 5.

32. Ibid.

Sally Brickman and Joanne R. Euster

Staff Relations

The library's public relations toward its own staff has many of the same objectives as client-oriented relations. It serves to tell the audience—in this case the staff—about the organization. A good, continuous system of staff relations also provides feedback, telling the administration what the staff at the operational level thinks about the organization and what it needs. Feedback also helps planners and organizers understand what is needed to obtain the goodwill or cooperation of staff. Based on that feedback, the complete staff relations system plans and carries out the means of winning and utilizing that cooperation.

Staff commitment to library goals and objectives and to seeing them carried into action should be the desired result of the staff relations program. The ultimate result to be sought is the delivery of excellent library service. Conscious, systematic intramural communication enhances the views of staff members about the importance of their own jobs and those of their colleagues and leads to operational improvements by coordinating the staff members' ideas of better library service with the library's goals and objectives.

Consequently, positive staff relations depend upon a strong communication process. This process requires that communication flows in many directions—top to bottom, bottom to top, and laterally between units.

Depending on the size and organization of the library, staff relations may be part of the total public relations role assigned to one librarian, it may be part of a broader administrative role, or it may be assigned to no one in particular, appearing as a function in the job description of all administrators or unit heads. The following section describes the role of the staff relations librarian as if that responsibility resided with one person. In libraries where this is not the case, the functions still need to be carried out, although they may be distributed among a number of individuals. It is important, however, that the responsibilities be made explicit, lest the adage "everybody's business is nobody's business" apply.

The Role of the Staff Relations Librarian

A staff relations librarian must be first and foremost a communicator. He or she must operate as a consultant who is knowledgeable about activities throughout the library and must be able to communicate, formally and informally, with each staff member, with the library's administrators, and with the library's constituents. Most staff relations librarians work toward the following objectives:

1. To create among all staff an awareness of the library's goals and objectives
2. To keep staff informed of events within the library and those events that affect them from the outside
3. To try to increase the effectiveness of all staff as library ambassadors, on and off the job
4. To encourage positive and constructive work attitudes among the staff
5. To establish and facilitate a communications network within the library that allows for downward, upward, and lateral exchanges of information.

Central to all of these objectives is the importance of personal contact between the librarian responsible for staff relations and the individual staff members.

The staff relations librarian must listen. Constant "keeping in touch" means that the librarian knows who is responsible for what and who is excited about what. To communicate effectively, the staff relations specialist must know about all aspects of the library. Staff must be reminded to keep him or her up to date, so that each staff member's services, programs, and plans can be communicated to other staff, to the administration, and to library users. Because the staff relations librarian usually has other public relations reponsibilities as well, the staff will see that informing the staff relations person will also mean that the library's constituents are well informed.

Information dissemination of this kind takes a great deal of time. However, there are numerous formal devices and systems which facilitate the information flow.

The Staff Newsletter

The newsletter is a basic device for staff communication; it can contain both official communications and relatively informal material. The newsletter thus serves both to keep people up to date and as a record of the in-house activities of the library.

New policies and procedures of the library, such as personnel procedures and announcements, are important, as are the announcements of new services and calendars of upcoming events.

Contents of a less formal nature can add to the newsletter's value and interest to staff. Interviews with staff members, new and old, provide an opportunity to inform staff of library activities. At the same time, the interview gives the staff relations person a chance to know staff members better.

Regular publication and distribution simultaneously throughout the library's departments contribute to the newsletter's credibility. These features, combined with thoroughness in its contents, make the newsletter an important resource for staff, helping to avert the "nobody ever tells me" syndrome.

Other Written Communications

The newsletter, of course, only supplements the other written communications of the library. Others include the formal mechanisms whereby employees are informed of basic working conditions, hours, paydates, personnel policies, parking regulations, and other details. This category also includes routine announcements and reminders as well as formal statements of policy and procedures. The procedures manual, usually in loose-leaf format to provide for frequent updating, records the day-to-day standards of each department, as well as its goals and objectives. *Staff Communication in Libraries* by Richard Emery (Linnet, 1975) is perhaps the classic handbook on the organization and importance of such communication.

The staff relations specialist should be alert to the problems of these ongoing systems of written communication. Once they are set up and operating, people tend to assume that they are self-perpetuating. A second problem is that such systems usually affect mostly communication from the top down. Positive steps will be needed to ensure that these systems continue to function—that is, that new employees receive adequate orientation, that news regularly finds its way into the newsletter, that new material continues to be filed in the procedures manuals, and that channels of communication in other directions are kept open as well.

Special Projects and Meetings
The staff relations effort, directed at enhancing communication among the staff, will demand the involvement of the staff relations librarian in the planning processes of the lirary and its departments. The librarian is likely to find himself or herself involved in search committees, staff development planning committees, library orientation, and recruitment.

Special projects, long-range planning, and broad self-studies, such as those demanded for membership in the Association of Research Libraries, place special burdens for internal communication on the library and call upon the talents and expertise of the staff relations specialist. Lateral and upwards communications are especially important if these activities are to succeed. It is a difficult task to determine how often and in what detail a departmental committee or subcommittee should issue a memorandum to the director and/or a general announcement to the library. It is similarly important to learn at what point to ask another department or committee to send a representative to a meeting when overlapping responsibilities appear. Good staff relations work will provide for informal communications in all directions and alert staff members to the right times for more formal communication.

Special Meetings
Several types of meetings are especially important to good staff relations. First are staff development and informational meetings at which library staff learn about the operations of other departments and the library in general.

A second kind of special meeting is the retreat, a day or weekend spent by most or all of the library staff away from the library. Usually the retreat has a single broad topic, such as closing the card catalog, book preservation, the genesis of a book, information retrieval systems, or a review of library planning and procedures. A different group of staff members may plan each retreat. Plans should include time for recreation as well as for the business at hand. Workshop sessions composed of smaller departmental groups, combined with the activities of the group as a whole, should aim at creating a linked system of the entire staff and their responsibilities. The retreat, more than any other single activity, can foster a sense of common cause in the library.

Staff Relations: An Open System at Work
What does a comprehensive staff relations program look like in practice? The following case study is drawn from actual experience in an academic library.

First, last, and always, management and staff talk to each other informally through personal contacts and an open-door management policy. The open door and willingness to talk never imply, however, violation of the chain of command or the ability of a staff member to go over the supervisor's head on functional matters. Informal communication takes up a lot of management time, but it ensures that everyone knows what is going on and gives a sense of others being aware and interested.

On a more formal level is a system of written policies and procedures. A loose-leaf manual, organized by topic and located in every department, is updated and revised regularly. Most other written communications are in the form of general staff memos, meeting minutes, and circulated copies of other important policy documents, as well as a regular newsletter.

The heart of this system of staff public relations—defining public relations not only as communication but also as a system of winning and developing goodwill and commitment—is embedded in the library's planning and evaluation process. The process involves two critical elements: first, participation in planning and evaluation; and second, widespread understanding of both the process and the plans developed.

All staff members and departments of the library are involved in planning. The process can be visualized as a pyramid, at the top of which is the statement of philosophy and goals of the library. Developed by the library faculty, this statment is coordinated with the university's goals statement and is periodically revised.

One level down the pyramid is the library's three-year plan. This plan, developed by a committee of library administrators, faculty, support staff, and students, is reviewed and approved by the University Planning Council. It includes detailed planning for library programs, including costs and implementation timelines, and it is directly related to the library statement of philosophy and goals.

At the pyramid's third level is the annual budget submission and a set of annual objectives for the library and its departments. All levels of staff participate in budget planning and the final document is circulated to all departments for information and review. Annual objectives are developed with the same high level of staff input and are written using a modified management-by-objectives approach.

Finally, the broadest level of the pyramid is composed of each staff member's individual objectives. These are mostly self-designed and are included as the self-evaluation section of the annual performance evaluations.

To provide a link between personal and departmental objectives, a day-long workshop for the entire staff is held annually. Meeting away from the library and focusing entirely on planning, the staff considers an agenda which includes the goals statement, the three-year plan, the annual budget, and overall annual objectives. Library planning and the entire university's planning and budget cycles are reviewed. Small departmental groups meet in workshop sessions to develop a prioritized list of one-year objectives for each department. Finally, individuals work on their separate objectives. At every step the emphasis is on creating a *linked* system.

Meetings are essential for adding a time dimension to the communications system. They are the most important means of maintaining continuity throughout the planning cycle. A system of committees, task forces, and departmental meetings provide for staff input, interdepartmental communication, and heightened awareness of what is of concern at present. Large group meetings of the library faculty, the support staff organization, and the entire staff are held for library-wide information dissemination, although at less frequent intervals.

This system, briefly described here, works well. It has resulted in excellent morale. Change is readily accepted and fairly easily implemented. Productivity is high. Because of good staff relations, the library is able to operate as an expanding organization, with all the energy, creativity, and enthusiasm that implies.

Conclusion

What is it that we want from staff relations? Basically, we want two things. We want people to feel good about their work, a human need. We want them to do their work well, an organizational objective. To meet the first need, we must ensure that each staff member is included and respected and feels that his or her work makes a valued contribution to the organization. On the organizational level, to do the job well, each staff members needs to have enough information to understand the job he or she does and how the job fits into the overall goal of the library and of the university or other institution or agency. In addition, each staff member needs to have a means of communicating with management to share needs, concerns, and ideas.

The effective staff relations program is in part an activity and in part an organizational style and philosophy. Free flow of information certainly can be systematized, but to make it work, the underlying principle must be a certain permeability of the organization to new ideas and a basic assumption that the sharing of information is good for the library.

Dawn Heller and Ann Montgomery Tuggle

Planning for Public Relations in the Media Center

"Doing the right thing—and letting people know about it" is really what good public relations is all about for all types of organizations. Trying to have good public relations without having a solid program of resources and services is madness. Public relations without a program is like waving your arms in the air for attention with nothing to merit that attention.

Consequently, we are assuming that in your school library media program you are trying "to do the right thing," and that you would like to improve your communications in order to let others know of your services and your value to the people you serve. There is a logical process that can be followed in order to plan for your improved communications, which we recommend. This planning process is the model developed by the National School Public Relations Association (NSPRA) and used in their building-level school communications workshop kit. Although this model was developed for the school media center and will use examples from it, its procedure may be adapted to many other situations.

IDENTIFYING THE PUBLICS TO BE REACHED

Just who are the "publics" served by the school media program? Obviously, we serve several groups of clients. It may help to think of these publics in two categories, internal and external.

Internal publics are those people within the school district or perhaps even within a single school building. Students,

Parts of this selection have also appeared in *Media Spectrum* 8:2 (1981).

teachers, department heads, and administrators are all obvious publics. But others should be considered as internal publics as well; these include the board of education, and the custodial, cafeteria, and secretarial staffs (incidentally, research has shown that the two most believed staff members in a school are the secretary and the bus driver, so it isn't farfetched to want to communicate with them). Other groups, such as substitute teachers, student teachers, the parent-teacher organization, and the school "boosters" club, may be important, too.

The external publics have relationships with the library that are relatively indirect. For a school media center, these could be community residents with no school-age children; the business community and civic organizations; the mass media; the city, county, state, and federal government officials who represent our district; the staffs of other types of libraries; the vendors who serve us; and the like.

After completing a thorough inventory of your potential publics, you should go on to rank the specific publics with whom you wish to improve communication. Perhaps the most important will be the media center student aides, mother volunteers, science teachers, or the principal. The library media center staff must identify the groups with which you are most eager to improve relations.

Once you have targeted a "public," you are ready to move to the next phase of the needs assessment process. You and the rest of the staff should ask yourselves two questions: (1) Why should we communicate with this "public?" and (2) What does this "public" need to know about our media program? Your answers will form the basis of your public relations, or P.R., plan. By answering, you will be able to focus on the most important information you wish to transmit or the attitudes you wish to change.

MASS AND INTERPERSONAL COMMUNICATIONS

Now you are ready to consider the varieties of ways that *might* be employed in your communications plan for your selected public. There are two broad categories in communications techniques. The first, *mass* communications, has as its main strength the transmission of information. In this category we can place all types of print, such as flyers, announcements, memos, and news releases. In addition, speeches and audiovisual presentations to an audience are also mass communications techniques. The second category is *interpersonal* or *face-to-face* communication. Included here are dialogues, conferences, telephone conversations, workshops, retreats, seminars, and social activities. These types of communication are best used for changing attitudes; this is, in fact, their key function.

When planning a P.R. project, you will want to consider both mass media and interpersonal communication techniques, selecting those that are most feasible and appropriate for your public and your purpose. Now consider the ways you can improve two-way communication with this public. It is best at this point to really brainstorm and list all kinds of ideas, even if they seem a little far-out or crazy. A group brainstorming will often come up with new and unique approaches. Once a list of ideas has been compiled, go back and select those ideas that seem to offer the best opportunities for success. Make sure that you have selected the appropriate mix of interpersonal and mass communications.

FEEDBACK

A final consideration in your preliminary planning must be that of *feedback*. Since communications is a two-way process, it is critical to think about ways of listening to the publics you serve. Feedback methods can also be divided into mass communication and interpersonal communication. On the one hand, you may wish to distribute a questionnaire widely to all parents in the district to get responses. Or you may want to seek one-on-one feedback, perhaps through conversations with teachers working with you on a special curriculum project. Again, the choices depend upon your target public and the purpose of your communications project. Your feedback choices must be selected to provide you with the information you need to determine if you are succeeding in communications efforts.

With the foregoing you have an overview of what is needed for a P.R. communications project. NSPRA's model suggests six components for a successful outcome:

1. A brief statement of the project (who and what)
2. Purpose of the project (why)
3. Procedures to be utilized (how)
4. Resources to be utilized (with)
5. Timing of the project (when)
6. Assessment (with what results)

Step 1. Briefly state the project. Here's where we delineate—in brief terms—what we hope to accomplish. We should keep our project concept short, sweet, and achievable. This is not the total P.R. program; it is a step, one aspect we are activating through a carefully thought-out plan. The project we will use as an example may be the first in a sequence of projects for an overall program, or it may be one of several simultaneous steps. The key is that it is stated as what we want to do:

> To involve the principal and assistant principals in activities of the media center.

Step 2. Identify the purpose(s) of project. While in the first we identified *what* we are going to do, in this step we indicate *why* we're going to do it. We identify for ourselves the hoped-for outcome of our activity. To some of us, this actually may be the first step. We may state "because I want *x*, I will do *y*." But, if we follow the NSPRA system, we're saying "I will do *y* because I want *x*."

The order, of course, is not as important as the outcome. Why do we want to do anything? Again, our why should be short on philosophy and long on practicality, in this instance:

> To involve the administration in a more active role within the center so they will begin to identify with it.
> To increase the administration's understanding of the center's program.
> To obtain feedback from the administrators about what they see, learn, and regard as the center's activities.
> To obtain administrative support for the media center's program.

Step 3. Procedures. Here's the "really big one": the *how*. If we do *y* because we want *x*, we still have to tackle *z*—the way we will proceed. Again, we need to be practical: we must analyze what we can do and then select from that the things we can do well. We cannot tackle everything; we must not program ourselves for failure. We're still operating in the achievable sphere. We're still recognizing that this step is just part of an overall program.

We should make this part of the plan detailed enough to keep us on target, to be sure our procedures move forward, even if there are times we don't seem to be moving.

At this point, it's worthwhile to note that development of this project should include all staff. All clerical and/or professional staff should be involved in the brainstorming, which is vital in this step. You may identify steps 1 and 2, but all the diverse ideas (and subsequent assistance because of involvement) will make this third step truly worthwhile. By involving staff in the how, you're not only recognizing their talents, their ideas, and their own unique knowledge, but you're also making use of them advantageously.

> Compile a list of possible activities in which the administration could be involved. Begin with activities you currently do, then add new ones you could try.
> When you have the entire list, select those you feel would present the media program at its best, and those you feel the administration would be willing to do.

If you're adventurous, take a chance and develop some really significant as well as some fun-oriented activities. For example, let's say there's some legislation pending in your state that could affect libraries—or maybe school library/media center membership in library systems is a big item—why not gather the information about these issues and present it to the appropriate administrators in your school. Tell them what's happening and ask for their input. Point out the effect on the school's media program. Then ask for their help. Draft a letter of support or concern and ask the administrators to sign it.

Too often we bemoan administrative indifference to concerns and developments affecting our programs, yet we never bother to inform or involve administration sufficiently. Often a recognition on our part that the administration might be interested in these issues results in a recognition on their part that there is more to our program than checking materials in and out.

Here are some other ideas to encourage an administrator's involvement in your program. If an administrator plays golf or has another hobby, why not use him or her as a subject for a demonstration on use of video equipment? The demo could show the teaching aspect of video tape—how doing, reviewing, and redoing increases skill. Or it could show people how to use the equipment. Or the activity could spin off into a program. "Here's how one golfs; here's what you need to know/do/have; here are some good materials on the topic." The list of possible activities could go on and on. To mention just a few:

Ask administrators to list their favorite books; then take their pictures and feature them and their favorites in a bulletin board display.

Compile a monthly chatty report of what's going on in the media center, identifying who's working with what materials. Star any particularly ambitious project and ask the principal to sign a "happygram" (designed by you), which will go to the teacher, noting his or her project.

Ask the administrators to judge any contests you may have and have them, not you, sign and confer awards.

Send the administrators a response form to suggest ways your program could become more involved in upcoming school activities. Then plan a follow-up conference to discuss it.

Ask the administrators to review your script about the school for a slide/tape program. Develop several multimedia shows about various school programs and seek administrative assistance in editing and critiquing each one.

Seek out your principal in the fall and review your plans for the year's media program. Meet again at least twice during the year to review progress. Near the end of the year, summarize what happened and present ideas for the next year. Encourage reaction, discussion, and suggestion from your principal.

Plan a media aide lunch to honor those helpers who've done that "above and beyond" type of work. Invite the building administration to attend and address the group. Or make it a breakfast . . . or have one every month to honor the media aide of the month.

Ask the administrators to assist you or relieve you—for one period—so they can analyze firsthand how things function and make suggestions for improvements.

Ask the principal to send notes of appreciation to your volunteers. You can write them; have the administrator sign them.

Ask the administrators to introduce a unit from their subject speciality to a class . . . with your assistance.

Just remember, your project is involvement of the administration. You are seeking ways to get the administrators into your center and to make them aware of what's happening.

Step 4. Resources. Now you are ready to identify all the items and people and finances you will need to implement your chosen activities. You may need a form, a video tape, an assistant, whatever. Look at each chosen activity, analyze what you'll need, and write it all down.

Step 5. Timing. To keep on track, establish a timeline that indicates when you'll start each aspect of the project and when you'll finish. If this is a year-long campaign, you'll need to indicate in which month you'll do which activity.

Step 6. Assessment. Evaluate whether you involved the administration and, if you did, how effective that involvement was. One method is to give your administrators a reaction form and have them tell you how they felt and if they've changed their attitude toward the program or increased their knowledge of it. Another way is to interview them, either in person or by proxy. A final technique might be to keep track of whether you see or hear from the administrators more often. Or you might note if they seek you out for reports on the center's activities, or if they miss doing some of the things you'd initiated.

This six-step process describes the NSPRA method. It is effective and workable. All you need to do is commit the time and the thought to develop, implement, and evaluate it. It isn't, of course, enough to plan well without implementing that plan. Ask yourself, "What will we do Monday morning? What will we do by the end of next week? What will we do before a month goes by? How will we check our progress after three months?"

It is all too easy to become discouraged if you try to be everything to everybody at all times. Cut the loaf one slice at a time. Choose your target publics carefully, focusing first on the one that you feel is most critical. Remember, this is like missionary work, you can't expect to "convert" everyone at once.

It is also important to select communication techniques that you are comfortable using. However, we urge you to push yourself into trying some new approaches so that you will grow and strengthen your skills.

Finally, get as many people as possible involved in the planning process. Seek help, not just from the media staff but from supportive students, teachers, parents, administrators, etc. That approach will help you develop communications projects that are sure to work—sharing your successes with the publics you serve.

Theresa M. Fredericka

The Case for Creative Programming in School Library Media Centers

CREATIVE PROGRAMMING: WHAT IS IT?

Creative program is merely "doing something with the stuff in your library media center." It's breathing life into the collection. It's promoting your program, your materials, and your services. It's as elaborate as designing a spaceship for story hour or as simple as hosting a faculty craft display. It's showing the administration, teachers, students, parents, and community that the school library media center does things like celebrating National Library Week with a contest, or holding a storytelling festival for sixth graders, or promoting a "Reading Squad" that reads to younger students or senior citizens.

Do you remember the courses you took in your library training? Probably these included selection, cataloging, reference, children's literature, administration. Was there anything in creative programming? If so, terrific! Unfortunately, not many of us have had a course in creative programming. This may be why, up to now, many school media librarians haven't considered programming a priority. But times are changing. More school media people are talking about programming and more are doing it. Even without training, most are successful in their attempts. They are borrowing ideas and techniques from public librarians who have been programming for years. School media librarians are beginning to discover success with creative programming for *all* levels, kindergarten through twelfth grade.

WHY DO IT?

Creative programming can help you reach out to new users and bring in new friends. It can help increase the use of your resources, especially those not frequently circulating. Programming gives the media center a new look; it gives the place a relaxed atmosphere. It shows the world that the school library media center does more than house books and filmstrips, babysit senior high study halls, or send out overdue lists. Creative programming is part of the territory of the school media librarian, who promotes the use of books and media, reading and learning. Creative programming helps you promote services to the school and the community.

With the financial crunch affecting us all, we can ill afford static library media programs. We can ill afford to hear a senior graduate brag, "School media center? Never visited it. Don't even know where it was." We cannot afford the teacher who admits, "I just send my students down to the library to get them out of my hair. Besides why should the librarian mind? She doesn't have anything else to do." Or, the public librarian who says in a community meeting, "I haven't met the school librarian. I have no idea what the school media program is like."

It's time to become more visible. And one way to be more visible is to create programs. Most students and teachers don't really care about the time you spend ordering books, cataloging them, keeping statistics. But they will care about your creative programming, especially if it is designed with them in mind.

HOW TO DO IT?

1. *Get yourself ready*. It has been said, "Fun is not a place you can drive to; it's an attitude within." How's your attitude? Your enthusiasm will be contagious and of utmost importance to success. Think positive, and take a deep breath.

2. *Set the atmosphere*. Your center must have a punch to it. Hang posters and pennants from the sky! Have daily surprises lurking about. Take time to create a warm, inviting atmosphere with bright colors, displays, and welcome signs.

3. *Capture an idea*. What would students in your school like (that wouldn't be c-o-r-n-y)? Borrow an idea or make one up. Brainstorm with teachers and students. Ideas are limitless, the only boundary your imagination. (Another boundary is, perhaps, your principal's permission. Remember to get an okay for all programs, especially those borderline wild ones.)

4. *Pick your season*. Whenever, whatever for. Beginners may want to stick to the tried and true occasions like National Library Week or Children's Book Week. But don't forget special school activities such as the Science Fair or International Day and community events like Heritage Week or the Apple Festival.

5. *Search out the talent*. You won't need to look too far for talent to help with the high school lecture series. Why not poll the faculty and invite them to lead discussions about hobbies, areas of interest? Needed prizes for contests are as close as your desk drawer (remember all those goodies you retrieved from the last library meeting?). Creative programming works on a limited budget . . . or no budget at all.

6. *Publicize to the maximum*. Appoint a student P.R. director and stand back. Encourage announcements over the public address system; the usual signs in the halls; a release in the school or local newspaper. Remember the radio—most stations love student-made announcements.

WHAT TO DO?

The following list of ideas, developed from conversations with librarians willing to share ideas, by reading professional literature, and through personal experience, may provide suggestions for your programming celebration. Pick and choose from among the themes and crazy ideas. Most all can be adapted for any level of school—primary, middle, junior high, high school. Remember your possibilities are boundless. Create your own happening and let your imagination run *wild*!

Ask your principal to schedule a *sustained silent read-in*. What is it? Everyone in the school stops to read. The principal, the teachers, the librarian, the clerk, the secretary (one school takes the phone off the hook), and the students.

Encourage everyone to come to the library to select a new book. They may read anything. Hold the read-in for twenty minutes or a half hour. Try it in the afternoon or the morning. Try both. Your response on all levels will be positive.

Send a letter to all the school board members saying "Happy National Library Week." Invite them to come visit your library media center. Thank them for their continued support.

Bulletin board ideas. Whichever crazy idea you decide on, prepare your zaniest bulletin board. Push the old fiction classics with "Tried and True. Check one out for you." Sports, golf and tennis anyone? "Add a new dimension to your summer."

Everyone loves a contest. Have a *faculty sweepstake contest.* Serve refreshments. Have teachers sign up a week ahead for a drawing. Everyone registers and before the event, you explore your cabinets for appropriate prizes for each teacher. Examples: a worn-out filmstrip for the teacher who chews up the audiovisuals; a withdrawn 1942 book on grooming goes to a good sport who will appreciate your sense of humor. Other prizes—one free Xerox copy, one free slide, one private inservice lesson on the use of the videotape recorder (for the audiovisual hater), a free Coke, a stapler for the one who can't live without yours, etc.; sprinkle the above with bookmarks, paperbacks, I.O.U.'s for bibliographies, and so forth and so on. Each name drawn receives just the "right" prize.

Hold student contests. Offer "good egg" awards. Everyone not on the overdue list gets a good egg (a name tag shaped like an egg). Let everyone have a chance to bring in his or her overdue books and have the students wear their eggs a second day. You'd be surprised how fast good eggs can become items for the black market.

Hold an annual storytelling contest. Reinstate the folk-tale tradition. Train children in the art. Competition could be building level or district-wide.

Consider a contest for tall tales. The best excuse for why a book was overdue should prove entertaining and very interesting.

Sponsor a book-stacking contest. Have each homeroom send a representative. Too many homerooms? Elect one from each grade to compete. Videotape the action to share with the entire school.

Other contest possibilities: Draw five names at random from the daily circulation card file. Guess how many miles the librarian walks a day? Crossword puzzle and hula hoop contests. Prizes: lunch with the librarian; tee-shirts; Guinness Book of World Records; McDonald's gift certificates; record albums.

Sponsor a book fair; host a film festival. Invite students to show homemade 8mm movies. (You may want to preview these!) Take a book survey. Have the entire school choose a favorite book.

Sponsor informal discussion sessions. Topics? Motorcycle repair (bring the bike, too); a folksinger; local candidates for office; talk about saving money, nutrition, the pros and cons of jogging; a demonstration of ballet, potter's wheel, or any art form. Why not invite a local artist to work for a day or two in the library?

Take time to make a sign for your library media center. Put up a "welcome" sign. Hang those directional signs for Dewey numbers, the reference collection, the pencil sharpener. What about a "Please bother me for information" sign? Your name sign? A name sign for the clerk?

Give your best teacher or student user a "You're at the top of the stack" award. Make a special sign for your supportive principal or superintendent. Call in the newspaper—at least the school paper.

Hold a reading marathon on the courthouse steps. Attach a microphone and loudspeakers to the podium and invite community groups to read for designated hours nonstop. (One Kentucky county did it for twenty-eight hours straight with 153 readers, 21 clubs and organizations participating.) Why not try it in the school gymnasium?

"Hug a Book" Week. Another county in Kentucky built a twelve-foot thermometer for the County Board of Education's lawn. Teachers in all schools reported the number of books read during the special week. The public library added to its circulation. Daily counts were taken and marked on the huge thermometer for the entire community to see. A contest was held via the local radio station to guess the number of books read in the county. Grand total for one week: 76,453.

"Clone" on the catalog. One librarian built an alter-ego after reading the *National Geographic World*'s article on "How to Build a Dummy That Looks Like You." The clone sits on the card catalog reading "her" favorites. Students snatch the selections away. What a display!

Create a mile-long bookworm. Each child who reads a book during a special reading event gets to contribute to the bookworm that stretches one mile down the highway near the school. Caution: invite the State Patrol to help monitor the construction.

Balloon launch. Student places a slip of paper inside a balloon. The slip contains the title of a favorite book and the student's name and address and asks the receiver to reply with his or her favorite book! Finneytown Elementary, in Cincinnati, Ohio, reported one response returned eight months after the takeoff.

Take a book to lunch. Students reading after meal time receive a special certificate: "Certificate for ————." (Let your imagination be your guide.)

No time for writing bibliographies? Have your students create short five- to ten-title bibliographies on the topic of your/their choice. Have them shape and decorate according to topic, such as sports books in the shape of a sneaker, cooking books in the mold of a mixing bowl.

Telephone an author. Arrange for a conference call to the school's favorite author. Get a company or corporation in town to defray the expense.

Organize a "reading squad" of interested students, teachers, community members, senior citizens. Have the squad visit other grades or shut-ins.

Have a "Love Your Library" Week. Ask students to shower you with plants, art work, old paperbacks, original literary pieces, small pets (just how brave are you?). Remember those thank you notes for everyone.

Be lovable yourself. Give away kisses (the candy kind), hugs, bookmarks, bibliography to your best teacher utilizer. Hold a mercy moment for that "horrible-fines-always-offender."

Honor a special group each day for a week. Monday—students; Tuesday—teachers; Wednesday—support staff; Thursday—principal; Friday—school board members.

Establish a "Principal's Reading Club." Encourage children to join and read books. The child reading the most books wins the chance to be principal for an hour, or at least maybe lunch with the principal?

Create a "Teachers read, too" bulletin board. Have all faculty members share their favorite title with the school.

Plan a program; try some of these ideas! Creative programming will add visibility to your media center program, encourage use of library materials, bring people to your door, and guarantee a more well-rounded, popular media center program of service.

Maria Hayley

Promote Young Adults to Promote Young Adult Services

Public relations, like charity, begins at home. Is anybody home in your library? "The *librarian* is the library, after all, otherwise a vending machine would do."[1] You, the librarian, are the center of any P.R. project. Everything and everyone else connected with it is merely an extension of you, like the ripples reaching the far shores of a river are an extension of the stone thrown with force on its waters. You promote by doing and being. You are both the artisan and the tool, the arm and the hammer. As the artisan you direct the course of your "tools"—yourself, your people, your products. As the tool you lend yourself—your presence, personality, potential—to your own direction. Tools that best sculpt positive response are people tools. Begin with yourself. What you have and how you use it determines your success in assembling all the other "tools": teens, staff, community, etc. For instance, teens involved directly in planning and promoting their own programs almost always guarantee success. Involvement generates interest; interest generates audiences. The challenge is recruiting teens to participate in the first place. You have what it takes.

You have a face. Direct it to smile. "Practice in front of a mirror pleasant looks and friendly glances. (This presupposes you've practiced those pleasant thoughts and friendly feelings that make your smiles genuine.) The difference between a library that [draws] teens . . . and a library that repels them may be your face."[2]

You have a voice. Direct it to speak kindly, to ask: "May I help you? How do you feel about this? What do you think about that? What is your favorite book? What kind of activities would you like to see in this library? Would you like to be on our advisory council? Would you tell your friends?" Draw them out to draw them in.

You have maturity. Direct it to dignify your demeanor. Don't struggle to be cool, hip, hep, or anything else that feels too tight on your psyche. Sincerity's the thing that sends them in.

You have a counselor, for somewhere within you lives the teen you once were. Direct that teen to come out and work side by side with you daily, to teach you sympathy for the complex nature of the young adult, to flesh out the feel of adolescence. "Didn't you giggle? Didn't you cry easily? Didn't your palms sweat . . . when confronting an authority figure" who let you know that whatever it was you wanted to do had just better not be done in *this* library?[3] How did you feel about the adults in your life, your library, and why?

You have enthusiasm. You're excited about your product! You've planned a plush program—and you're not going to let it play to a puny audience.[4] No, never! Direct your enthusiasm to remove the ribbon from your gift of gab. Release it like bright balloons all over the library, then let it out into the community. Talk to everyone everywhere teens hang out—schools, shops, parks, clubs, etc.[5]—and you are guaranteed positive response, for armed with smiles, sincerity, sympathy, enthusiasm, and a live-in counselor on adolescent psychology, you become the greatest P.R. tool ever invented. Signs, posters, flyers, cards, letters, and telephone calls are merely an extension, a reinforcement, a souvenir of you. Your presence is what creates the real impact. Marshal this presence to recruit staff, administrators,[6] school personnel, youth workers, and community people. Involve them directly in some aspects of your program or service, and they will promote it because they have a personal stake in its success. (Remember the television commercial that ends with "And they told two friends and they told two friends, and so on, and so on, and so on . . . ?") Select them on the basis of their areas of expertise and apply that expertise where it will best further your promotional goals.

For example, the photographer would be the choice for taking publicity shots for a battle of bands contest, the president of the chamber of commerce for donating prizes, and the home economics class of Sweet Dreams High for baking the brownies to be gobbled at the victory celebration afterwards. Ask a little from a lot of people who are already good at what they do (you're a promoter, not a trainer) and the show will practically take itself on the road. The number and choice of people you recruit—not the amount of money you spend—is the primary factor in eliciting Positive Response.

Machiavelli, in his masterpiece *The Prince*, makes this point as it applies to war (you're fighting the war against apathy and empty libraries): "I maintain then, contrary to general opinion, that the sinews of war are not gold, but good soldiers; for gold alone will not procure good soldiers, but good soldiers will always procure gold." You can't buy a good audience, but you sure can raise one. Winston Churchill, referring to his country's role in World War II, put it another way: "Give us the tools, and we will finish the job." So, you've assembled your "tools," sharpened your skills, procured your "soldiers." Everyone is involved, raring to go. The work begins. Once recruited, participants must be guided to sustain that first high wave of enthusiasm. To keep teens interested in promoting your library, keep yourself interested in promoting your teens. (They are both your target and ammunition). It doesn't matter whether you're promoting your collection, your programs, or a service (it's a given you're pushing a good product), the main point is that you are promoting the teens' involvement with it.

When we asked our young adult advisory council to help us advertise our library's switch to Library of Congress classification from the Dewey system, they promptly created "Melville Who-o-o??"—a wise old owl feverishly fashioned during the afterschool hours in Ruth's garage from an old garbage drum, papier-mache, two paper plates, and the finest drops of paint left over from the ghosts of projects past. "Melville Who-o-o??" became an ambassador for the library and simultaneously raked in recognition for his creators, for Mel went on to win top honors as a high school homecoming float, marched in the community parades, appeared in Chicago's Grant Park at the ALA Centennial Conference, and had his portrait splashed on the post-conference pages of Library Journal and School Library Journal.

To advertise our young adult advisory council, we advertised the young adults in the council. Whenever they were involved in a library activity we photographed them (the camera was a bona fide member of the group) for feature articles in the local papers. They made personal appearances in library/community events. In "Uniform"—tee-shirts with the council's name on the front and the member's name on the back, and jeans—they became living posters, human banners proclaiming their support of the library, and the library's support of them. The council's president, Ruth Kutz, promoted our library and our council by speaking, in "uniform," at a program of the ALA Centennial Conference while fellow council members cheered on. They (plus over 100 other area teens) participated in all Young Adult Services Division (YASD) programs to demonstrate the division's conference theme, Celebrating Young Adults. Their names appeared on conference programs and in library publications.

One participating group of young muralists from Chicago's Public Art Workshop made the cover of *Top of the News*.[7] The council also made a page of *Seventeen* magazine.[8] And in the local post-conference paper, they were, of course, front-page news. None of this cost our library a dime (money was spent of course, but not ours—remember the "good soldiers" of Machiavelli), but the dividends were great. Our teens remained enthusiastic about their library and proved it by more than tripling attendance at library programs.

As with teens, to keep other "good soldiers" enthused about your library, promote their involvement with it and promote it often. When the manager of our local McDonald's offered to donate hamburgers, fries, and cokes for "some" library event, we didn't just take it sitting down amidst soft whispers of "thank you very much." No, indeed! We marched our youth council down to the Golden Arches, munched and malted on site, snapped photos of the kids smiling in front of the big "M" (say "cheeseburger"), and appeared in print the next Wednesday under the following caption: "Teens Meet at McDonald's to Plan Library Photo Contest." Needless to say much more "gold" came from McDonald's, in the form of food, fun, and prizes for the above-mentioned photo contest. To promote the library and in the same breath promote those who support it is effective in sustaining that support because the promotion acts as a reward and rewards reinforce. Sometimes, as in this case, public relations means promotional reinforcement. The reinforcement, however, must be repeated often. Many good beginnings die for lack of it. As Jacqueline Susann said, "Once is not enough."

The "people" principles of public relations mentioned in this article were branded on my mind early in my work with young adults. I applied them to pull our first photo contest from the flames of failure so that instead of cinders, I found success. I know that every librarian who wants teens in the library can do so by putting them first in his or her heart.

NOTES

1. Carol Starr, *Young Adult Alternative Newsletter* 1, no. 1: 3(1978).

2. Ann Osborn, "It's Not Enough to Love Books, Ya Gotta Love People, Too," *Library Journal* 98: 974–78 (1973).

3. Ibid.

4. For overviews of successful young adult programs, see Mary K. Chelton, "YA Programming Roundup," *Top of the News* 32, no. 1: 43–50 (November 1975); and Donna Meyers et al., "YA Programming Roundup II," *Top of the News* 32, no. 4: 81–88 (Fall, 1978).

5. "Be just as snoopy as a detective in finding these places," is the advice given (along with pages of suggestions and procedures) in *Look, Listen, Explain: Developing Community Library Services for Young Adults*, prepared by the Committee on Outreach Programs for Young Adults, Young Adult Services Division, American Library Association (Chicago: American Library Assn., 1975).

6. They may require special convincing. See "How to Win Friends and Influence Administrators," by Regina Minudri, *School Library Journal* 22, no. 5: 33 (January, 1976).

7. *Top of the News* 32, no. 4 (June, 1976).

8. "All Booked Up," *Seventeen* 32: 64 (April, 1978).

Pat Hogan

Library System's Role in Public Relations

The concept of a library system has been general and somewhat imprecise. The history of public library service, as reflected in such works as Carleton B. Joeckel's *Government of the American Public Library*, shows that there has long been a search for a unit of service larger than the municipal or city library.[1] The need has sometimes been filled by a county or multicounty library, a special district library, or a state supported library system (public library system).[2] The trend toward systems has been encouraged by the desire and need to offer a variety of services to participating libraries from a centralized structure. For some systems in the United States, system services consist of interlibrary loan arrangements and little else. For others, where library service is still undeveloped, the system, with its staff of professional librarians and other specialists, is seen as the provider of services. And in areas with more developed libraries, the system staff can be facilitators, by suggesting avenues for action, answers to questions, or approaches to resources of a higher or more sophisticated nature. For this last type of library (which usually is involved in its own intense P.R. program) the system in some instances must compete for attention to its activities. Depending on the nature of the system, the kinds of libraries that have joined to form it, and the services it offers to and for them, the P.R. package will focus to a greater or lesser degree on some or all of its constituents—other libraries and librarians, trustees, as well as the different public(s) of the member libraries. An examination of some approaches in public library systems in Illinois, their plans, use of publicity, and marketing of system services, will suggest what public relations in a system is and can be.

For the purpose of this paper, a public library system will be defined as a cooperative agreement of public libraries to exchange designated materials and achieve, through cooperation, a greater level of service to the patron. Public relations is defined as the sum total of skills, including planning, publicity, research, measurement/evaluation, and analyses, designed to reach many publics for the purpose of gaining total support and interest from the users for the system.

With these definitions in mind, we can describe system services, service recipients, and the ways to educate users about the services. System services may include interlibrary loan, reference, programs for the blind and physically handicapped, centralized acquisitions and book processing, centralized cataloging, bookmobile delivery, special collections, workshops and other continuing education activities, consultant service (on issues from the renovation of a building to the planning of a successful referendum), and van delivery service. The size of the staff may vary from several individuals to many in different departments. Titles may be descriptive, such as a head of reference, and may differ in meaning from system to system. Thus, the special services librarian or consultant may be involved in outreach or extension services or concentrate on one group (institutions, for example).

Few systems have the financial means to support a full-time P.R. staff position. Many assign the duties to a member staff officer who has both the ability and time to handle the responsibilities along with other duties. Others contract with outside agencies for specialist work, for example, for the design of a select type and number of brochures. Public relations may be assigned to a nonlibrarian on the staff. One recommendation has been to distinguish functions to be performed by professional librarians from functions to be performed by other professionals with management skills.[3]

And yet, public relations plays an on-going role in system activity, if only indirectly. The system, through its staff, goes into the library community, which is a service area that may range from several hundred to several thousand square miles in area and with a clientele similar in size to that of a small- to medium-sized public library or as large as the city of Chicago. It would be helpful to think of the system's clientele as if it occupied concentric circles, with the system headquarters as a center.

COMMUNICATING WITH MEMBER LIBRARIES

The first client community (and, indeed, literally, the system) comprises the libraries, with their administrators, staffs, and trustees. With their help and information, the system was created with a designated range of services. The next consists of the administrators, who work with staff and/or the public to implement system services. But, in addition, they also are the recipients of system continuing education efforts and are participants in system legislative or long-range planning efforts. Therefore, they stand in a unique position, between the library per se and the secular patrons, as both participants/distributors of the P.R. message and, as individuals, specialized patrons/users of the services that the system offers.

Print

A newsletter is one means of getting the message to an individual library so that an awareness of and use of the system's services can take place. A system newsletter, whether booklet or legal-sized handout, and whether monthly or bimonthly, usually describes ongoing professional activities (national, state, or local programs or conferences), articles or books of professional interest and material or information from the system on grants, cooperative purchasing opportunities, or legislative updates, for example. In some cases the system will provide information on items for sale or give-away, or on job openings. The newsletters are distributed to the head librarian or administrator of the public or nonpublic library with copies as requested to library board members. And some newsletters have been quoted in the national library press (excerpts from the *Nor'easter* of the North Suburban Library System have been credited in *LJ Hotline*, for example). In these days of restricted funds and the mandate to avoid duplication of services as well as materials, the system can be perceived as a strong resource that supplements local efforts and that relies on cooperative exchange of materials so that everyone can benefit. System public relations thus engages the audience in a two-fold relationship and it "sells" its product or service while promoting a concept(s)—such as sharing or cooperative borrowing (or planning or programming).

Media

Film, videotape, and cassettes are among the media that can be effectively used to tell the system's story. One of the most interesting examples of a way to tell this story is a three-part film of system services prepared for the North Suburban Library System (NSLS), Wheeling, Illinois, by Industrifilms (Hawthorn Woods). The film incorporates a fictional setting (though based on real situations) and system personnel, photographed in their units, to illustrate behind-the-scenes activities of each system service (in this case, reference and centralized serials). The film then is booked by each requesting library to be used in-house for staff training or for a library board meeting. By explaining the activities and concepts to the local library staff, the system strengthens the bond for local promotion of its services.

Workshops

Workshops for sharing ideas and distributing information packets easily fall within the purview of systems public relations. At the Lincoln Trails System (Champaign, Illinois), resource sharing among school media specialists was one target group promoted by the system as part of its commitment to nonpublic libraries in its area. A special packet of information was prepared and distributed to libraries and school media centers. In another effort to help local libraries, the Starved Rock Library System (Ottawa, Illinois) has held workshops on ideas to use in holiday programs.[4] Metropolitan systems such as the NSLS, DuPage, and the Suburban Library Systems have held workshops, prepared press releases, and regularly produce newsletters and weekly information sheets (such as the *Bulletin Board* in the NSLS).

COOPERATING WITH MEMBER LIBRARIES TO COMMUNICATE WITH THE PUBLIC

Public library systems also produce materials and programs aimed directly at library users and the general public. Brochures and posters are often prepared by systems because member libraries can share production costs by using such cooperative organizations. These jointly produced materials do not necessarily relate to system services; more often, they concern programs or services that any public library might offer.

Similarly, systems are often the most suitable facility for

public libraries to use in preparing general promotion campaigns. The systems give the libraries the advantages both of sharing costs and of speaking with unanimity. In the Chicago area, television sports were used to promote Dial-A-Pet and Dial-Law, (access by telephone to tapes on subjects of interest about law or about animals). The use of media in this endeavor was an instance in which the system's message was aimed directly at the public. But that public's inquiries and need for further information would be directed to each local library for answers, and, if necessary, to the system.

One system that identified in its public information office a strong commitment to public relations is the Chicago Library System (CLS), one of eighteen library systems in Illinois. CLS is a consolidated library system; that is, it consists of a central library with many branches, unlike the other seventeen library systems in Illinois, where different public libraries have joined to share resources. Since CLS is both a system and a large urban library, it needs effective public relations to highlight the distinct potential of its different service dimensions, as a system and as a large city library. CLS's public relations program involves the talents of a staff including a professional photographer and a graphics professional to put the media to good use in publicizing opportunities at the branches as well as at the Cultural Center for programs and services. Aided by a variety of media approaches, a strong staff, and an in-house graphics department, the Chicago Library System's P.R. program appears smart, savvy and on-target. The objectives of this department include the assignment of projects, creation of guidelines, and the channeling of publicity for each unit to the most appropriate medium. Such organization allows maximum coverage for all with a minimum of interlibrary competition for the same space or air time.[5] The director of media productions (formerly the director of broadcasting) handles all public service announcements including broadcast community calendars and all radio and television appearances. The weekly half-hour radio show, "Your Library Notebook," is devoted exclusively to showcasing programs, resources, and services. The P.R. office handles publicity for major special events. And a full-time photographer is available to take pictures of all Chicago Public Library-Chicago Library System events. Perhaps the most important guidelines that this office has written are the procedures for media relations in an emergency.

For the other seventeen library systems in Illinois and, indeed, for most other systems in the country, public relations probably takes a more humble form, but effectively and successfully.

At this time, it may be well to ask what systems can be doing (or planning to do) as libraries plan for the future. A *Library Journal Special Report* (no. 18), "Beyond PR: Marketing for Public Libraries," edited by Joseph Eisner, suggests in a number of its articles that the application of marketing techniques may help libraries meet the needs of the library user/consumer. Marketing audits, plans, and community analyses are approaches to identification of the library's marketplace. And a system's P.R. program, which can draw on a large base of people and combine the promotion, workshop, and planning processes, can be of enormous benefit to its member libraries. It suggests long-range P.R. planning, to be centrally produced and using marketing approaches. A system, already committed to cooperative endeavors and sharing ideas with its libraries, can build on this existing P.R. program foundation to help implement marketing techniques for the better promotion of itself and its libraries.

Public relations for systems will always have the power to be dynamic and to fulfill the definition of synergy, a smooth working together of parts large and small.

NOTES

1. Carleton B. Joeckel, *Government of the American Public Library* (Chicago: Univ. of Chicago Pr., 1934).
2. *Public Library Systems in the United States: A Survey of Multijurisdictional Systems* (Chicago: American Library Assn., 1969), p. 15.
3. Ibid., pp. 250–1.
4. Connie Etter, "The Datebook" *ILA Reporter* 7: (May-August, 1977).
5. Nancy Moss, "The Chicago Public Library Policy: Media Relations/All Public Service Units."

BIBLIOGRAPHY

Eisner, Joseph, ed. "Beyond PR: Marketing for Libraries." L.I. Special Report No. 18. New York: Bowker, 1981.

Etter, Connie. "The Datebook" Public Relations and Publicity Committee. Illinois Library Assn., (May-August 1977).

Gregory, Ruth, and Lester Stoffel. *Libraries in Cooperative Systems; Administrative Patterns for Service.* Chicago: American Library Assn., 1971.

Moss, Nancy. "The Chicago Public Library Policy: Media Relations (All Public Service Units)." In *Librarians Guide to Effective Public Relations*, n.d.

Rice, Betty. *Public Relations for Public Libraries; Creative Problem Solving.* New York: Wilson, 1972.

Sherman, Steve. *The ABC's of Library Promotion.* Metuchen, N.J.: Scarecrow Pr., 1980.

Part Three

Skills for
Public Relations

items to help you polish and make easier your artistic techniques. Everyone, even the pros, should spend more time here than they do. Become friends with the store clerks. Take an hour or so to look at and read about the products and supplies. Ask what's new. Ask what's easiest. Describe your graphics set up and ask which items will help you. The larger cities have really terrific art supply stores worth visiting on a trip if you're not from a metropolitan area.

Your own library is another great source for graphic design ideas. There's a wealth of inspiration in the stacks too fathomless to be specific about. A specific example is children's books, because they keep the points of communication simple. And simplicity is a key to good graphics.

Other libraries have your problems and solve them, often with great printed materials which will inspire you. Exchange sample packets of printed work on a regular basis with several other libraries. Ask if you may copy the pieces that will work for you.

GOOD GRAPHICS READING

Upper Case & Lower Case (quarterly). Full of great art and inspiration. Free if you order for your "art" or "printing" department! Contact: *Upper Case & Lower Case*, 216 E. 45th St., New York, NY 10017.

The Library Imagination Paper (quarterly). High quality, reproducible library clip art, how-to articles on graphics and library P.R. topics. $14.00 per year. Contact: Carol Bryan Imagines, 1000 Byus Dr., Charleston, WV 25311.

Dover Publications, Inc., 180 Varick Street, New York, NY 10014. This publisher offers more than 130 low-cost, beautifully prepared paperback books with copyright-free art, alphabets, and borders. Write for a catalog of titles.

Graphic art-trade publications. Borrow trade publications from an artist friends and pore over them. Send away for any free samples or product information offered. Some of the art trade publications are: *Art Direction, Graphis, Print*, and *Advertising Techniques*.

GOOD TRICKS TO KNOW

Poster lettering is no sweat when you use these two easy lettering styles (see figures 1 and 2). If you can print your name, you can dash off the Ball-Bearing or the Fat Chance alphabets like an expert!

Carol Bryan and Mona Garvey

The Goods on Graphics

This article assumes that you are a librarian who is expected to dabble in the graphic arts rather than a graphic artist who is expected to dabble in the library. But, if you *are* an artist, take a look anyway; you may find a new idea or two here.

While messing up on a third attempt in as many hours to do a piece of art or a paste-up for your library, do you think enviously of those graphic artists with years of technical training and loads of talent? You can close the frustration gap impressively by latching onto some of the tricks of the trade and learning how to get around in this weird and specialized area, tricks *all* trained artists learn and use! Even if you aren't expected to cut, paste, and paint, being aware of this collection of goodies will help you to communicate with artists and keep them happily at work for your library.

GOOD THINGS TO KNOW ABOUT GRAPHIC ARTISTS

Artists will give you better results if you give them time to think about a job. Graphic art is as much a mental process as it is a technical operation. The two parts working together add up to creativity—the bright idea. Even if you have only vague details of a far-in-the-future job, keep the artist informed so that the info can rumble around in the gray matter and explode into brilliance at deadline time.

Artists are more sensitive than most people by virtue of their profession. Their sensitivity is what makes them far better at being artists and far worse at accepting criticism. It's wise to remember this, and think up some tactful way of saying a piece isn't acceptable, or you'll never get a decent redo!

An isolated work area works miracles. Give them a place to concentrate and perform technical skills without distraction and you'll get better work and faster turn-around time for your money. Go look at some good art departments in your town and see how they are set up.

GOOD THINGS TO KNOW ABOUT GRAPHICS

Effective graphic art is usually achieved by expressing an idea in a direct and simple form. The art is not there simply to look pleasing, as is wallpaper, but to make a statement that persuades and inspires the viewer to take action. The art must do its job quickly and, therefore, simplicity is best. Even if you are able to find a very cluttered and busy piece of graphic art somewhere, it will be sending forth a singular, bold message if it is any good.

Color schemes in graphic art must also work to attract the attention of the public. You aren't color-coordinating an Easter outfit or a breakfast nook here; you're using color to make the viewer notice important information. Think in terms of what is striking rather than what is pretty when selecting colors.

Great graphic design occurs because it is inspired. Every artist has inspiration points. In no-nonsense language this could mean *idea files* labeled "people," "nature," "animals," etc. The artist keeps an eye out for appealing pictorial matter (in magazines, newspapers, greeting cards), clips and files it. It is not used as something to be copied, but to be looked at and adapted in the artist's own style. Inspiration points could also mean certain nonart subjects offering line and style. The beautiful positioning and motion of figure skating, ballet, and exercise can be very inspiring. Of course, music has always churned the creative juices. Turn on your favorite sounds and turn on!

GOOD PEOPLE TO KNOW ABOUT

The printer can save you a lot of up-front grief if you check with him or her first. Have the printer show you several pieces of camera-ready art and the finished printed piece for each, so that you can see how the results were mechanically prepared for printing by the artist. Ask questions about what you don't understand. Take notes. Ask if the printshop has any "set-up sheets" to get rid of, and you may go back to the library with a stack of "gold." Set-up sheets are papers used over and over to get the press lined up and in register to print a job. They have lots of colors and lots of designs from lots of jobs all over them.

These can be used for bulletin board, display, or poster backgrounds. If you really want to test your persuasive powers, see if the printer will part with a few sheets of pressure-sensitive paper. You can use this stick-back, bright colored paper as poster backgrounds and for spot color on numerous items.

The photographer can help you by turning your black and white lettering or artwork into tiny little negatives that can be slipped into slide mounts colored with special pens if you like, and flashed on the screen as titles, credits, or art "breaks" between the photo slides in your show. Be sure to do the art in proportion to the dimensions of the slide. The photographer can also put your logo on positive film in various sizes so that you can place it on top of screened photos or other art that goes on copy machine-produced materials.

The local artists in town might do some free work for you in return for an ego trip; you can offer them a one-person show of their work in your library. You'll publicize this, of course, so that the crowds will appear and marvel at the work on exhibit!

GOOD PLACES TO KNOW ABOUT

The newspaper is always the place to find a selection of clip art books. If you've done your P.R. homework, you'll certainly know someone there who can usher you into the nonpublic area where these volumes of ready-to-use art are kept and give you carte blanche clipping privileges. You will have to flip through life-size likenesses of chuck roasts to find the stuff you can use, but you won't be disappointed.

The supermarket offers spendid answers to your questions about effective use of color for promotional purposes. You know about those Madison Avenue surveys that give impressive statistics about colors of cereal boxes and how the ones with lots of orange and red sell better? Top dollars are paid by the food conglomerates to find out what attracts the public. So, even if you do buy the blue instead of the red box, walk the aisles! See what colors are most plentiful and prominent on the shelves and use them as your materials.

Any mother's refrigerator door proudly exhibits a gold mine of beautiful, straightforward, unabashed art done by her kids. Just the inspiration you need to get your art technique back to the carefree, "I am great" style we all shared as children, before we had been taught the "correct" way to draw a cow.

The art supply store holds many mysterious and wonderful

Fig. 1. The Ball-Bearing Alphabet
Reprinted from the Spring 1980 issue of *The Library Imagination Paper*.

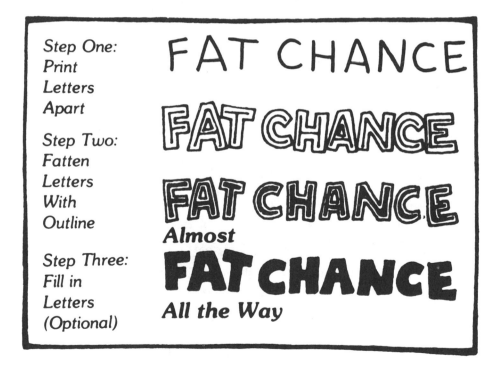

Fig. 2. The Fat Chance Alphabet
Reprinted from the Spring 1980 issue of *The Library Imagination Paper*.

Straight, even lettering without ruled pencil guidelines is a cinch with this method: Tape down a sheet of paper to your art surface to provide a straight edge. Hand letter or apply rub-down type about ¹⁄₁₆″ above the paper edge. (Why risk smears by having to erase pencil lines?)

Picking up rub-down type is easy when you make a mistake, and you won't scratch it into microscopic bits with this method: take a piece of Scotch Magic Transparent tape or Scotch masking tape and rub it down lightly over the letter, being careful not to let the tape touch any of the letters that are supposed to remain. The "mistake" will pull up easily, intact.

Gripper space is required by the printing press in outside border areas (unless it is a job that purposely bleeds off the edges). In preparing a job for the printing press, always leave at least ³⁄₈″ nonprint space around the outside edges.

Best paper sizes to plan standard printed work for are: 5″ × 7″, 8½″ × 11″, 8½″ × 14″, and 11″ × 17″. These sizes are readily available or usually cut without waste from most larger size stocks at the print shop. (You pay for any waste, even if you don't use it.) If an 8″ × 10″ flyer can just as easily be 8½″ × 11″, do it in that size so that standard paper can be used.

Flush left is better. Centering lettering on a hand-lettered job is a pain in the asterisk and not worth the time, unless you've got the experience to wing it, fudge it, and hope for the best. Do these jobs flush left (see figure 3) and save yourself a lot of grief.

Quick print and copy-machine printing. Be realistic about what results to expect from these methods and design for their limitations. It's best to avoid really bold type or solid ink coverage when doing work with paper masters instead of negatives and plates, or when using the copy machine for reproduction. Naturally, black ink is the only color that copies well.

GOOD ON-THE-SPOT DISPLAYS YOU CAN MAKE

Displays in libraries should have an informative message to deliver. This is especially true in smaller libraries where one person is often responsible for everything from reshelving books to library instruction to mounting displays. There simply isn't time to bother with "empty calorie" displays, which may look yummy but lack nutritional value. A "Spring into Spring" bulletin board may decorate a drab library but is unlikely to provide any educational nourishment. A "Facts about the Library"

FLUSH LEFT COPY   CENTERED COPY

Fig. 3. Lettering copy
Reprinted from the Spring 1980 issue of *The Library Imagination Paper*.

display, on the other hand, may be loaded with information but have the appeal of moldy bread. To be effective, most library displays should: (1) look good so folks will sample the content, and (2) have some content worth sampling.

Easily changed spot displays not only provide attractive formats for library related messages, but often suggest topics and approaches as well. Spot displays can help solve many patron information needs and pass on a smorgasbord of tidbits about library materials, services, programs, and usage. They are not, however, intended to be of the set-and-forget variety. Since these displays are designed for easy info changing, it's important to change messages often. If patrons see the same message week after week they'll quit looking and you'll have a stale counter sitter instead of an ongoing information display.

One of the easiest, most attractive, and most effective small displays is the typewriter cutout shown in figure 4. This display can be tacked to a small bulletin board, taped to a large

Fig. 4. Typewriter cutout spot display

bookend, or equipped with a prop back. The typewriter is sized to hold 8½″ × 11″ typing paper or notices and photocopies of similar size. Knobs, base, and paper support are cut from black poster board and glued to a piece of red-orange poster board. The 7″ × 12″ body of the typewriter is black poster board with keys, bar, and a piece of aluminum added ("TV dinner" thickness is about right). The body can be tacked in place or stapled along the bottom and sides; the top must be loose for insertion of paper.

Technical information. Except for the keys and bar, which can be cut from any white paper, use only poster board. The display is intended for long service and construction paper fades and tatters too quickly to be of any use. Use only rubber cement or a glue stick for attached pieces, because liquid glue runs, wrinkles paper, and generally messes up. Don't use a pastel color for the backing paper; use a bright color to contrast with a white paper insert. Since even careful scissor cutting leaves a rippled edge, poster board pieces will look better if cut on a paper cutter. Trace around a nickel for the keys (don't say we don't tell you everything).

The typewriter display can be used for news releases, budget figures, special interest bibliographies, subject headings and call numbers, book lists, book reviews, photocopies pages from reference sources—just about anything you want to explain or publicize. Branch or school libraries might make use of two typewriters, one for system news and one for local stuff. You might also tack one up in the faculty lounge, employee dining room, or hallway and insert regular news about library activities and materials.

Inserted sheets should be changed regularly to get and keep people in the habit of reading them. Interest will be hyped if sheets take a humorous and/or quiz approach. A multiple-choice quiz about library usage might include questions such as" "Are fiction books: A. Books by Billy Joe Fiction? B. Books about Bill Joe Fiction? or C. Made up stories?" Photocopies, pages from reference sources, literary classics, or current best sellers might ask patrons to pick the correct title amidst a list of outlandish choices. A Civil War bibliography might ask "Which of the following subject headings, call numbers, and choices have *no* relation whatsoever to the Civil War?" This single, easily constructed bulletin board prop provides a self-help aid, instructional sheet, and an attractive display all in one easy-to-change package.

An animal character (almost any animal will do) can introduce a series of them related or miscellaneous information. The orange "Wise Owl" in figure 5, for example, can inform patrons about: library usage ("Hey, don't forget to skip beginning 'A's and 'The's when you look for a title in the catalog"), favorite books and authors, useful reference sources, topical subject headings and call numbers, patron news ("Billy Soika's favorite call number is 796 and his favorite book is "The Mouse and the Motorcycle"), and library operation ("How much per day, per capita does the library cost taxpayers? A. 15¢ B. 7¢ C. 2¢").

Since the character's comments are printed in very simple, cartoon character "balloon" type, the information offered is easily changed. Even though making the change is easy, some thought has to go into what you're going to say and how. Keep the language conversational and use current slang, lots of dots and dashes, and a generally informal approach: "Hey there, bookies ... I've got some hot tips on Melvil Dewey's tricky number game." Toss in some no-fail quizzes: "Which of the following does the library have?" Then list three or four titles

Fig. 5. "Wise Owl" display

you do have along with a "ringer" to pique interests. This kind of thing has to be easy, loose, and fun, with the hard information slipped in unobtrusively.

This type of display can be as useful in special and academic libraries as it is in public and school facilities. The owl can offer miscellaneous messages or a series of thematic messages about library usage, materials, programs, costs, savings, magazine articles, reference sources, reference questions, plans, and setbacks. You might opt for two or three critters with each giving specialized information; a "catalog cat," for example, to explain the ins and outs of your book, card, or computer catalog.

Technical information. Keep shapes very simple and cut them from poster board. Use bright colors (no pastels) or cover the critter with fabric (even stripes, plaids, or polka dots may make an impact). A black wide marking-pen line adds design interest, especially if it's about ¼" to ½" inside the cut edge. Glued-on white eyeballs also add interest and any realia jazzes things up: flea collars, sunglasses, neckties, buttons, or a "pinkie" ring on the owl's toes; the sillier the better. Patrons often enjoy bringing in critter accessories, so encourage them to do so.

The display in figure 6 is especially handy, since it's free standing. The backing is red-orange poster board with a round head and rubber-cemented eyeballs and pupils (trace around a plate for the head and small lids for eyes). The book jacket, being too flimsy for stability, is wrapped around poster board folded as shown in figure 7. The flaps are glued or stapled to the back of the main piece.

Figure 8 uses the same head, but check figure 9 for its slightly more complicated fold. The open book is a poster-board piece 8½" high and 20" long; pages are 6¼" wide, sides 3", and flaps ¾". Dimensions can be changed but sides should project at least 3" for stability. The back piece for the display shown is 12" × 15" and that too can be changed, though a larger piece would require a "book" with wider sides.

Technical information. Poster board should be scored (cut lightly with a razor or sharp knife along a metal-edge ruler) before folding. You then fold *back* along the scored line. The

Fig. 6. Free-standing display with book jacket

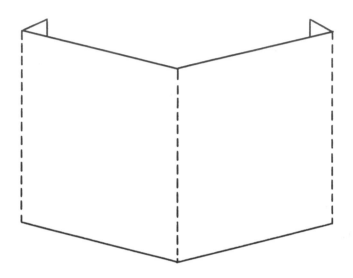

Fig. 7. Book jacket display

three cuts for figure 6 are all on the front, but the center cut for figure 8 is made on the back and the other cuts are made on the front. It's confusing, but you can work it out by trial and error. Note that the simple oval hands have a heavy marking pen line inside the edge. Hands are attached with rolled masking tape (or display putty or double adhesive tape) and they have to stick out to the side for maximum effect.

Figure 6 can be used as an attractive counter display piece, and information about books, authors, and programs can be added to the back of the book jacket. Figure 8 is even more useful because you can tack or rubber-cement book lists and photocopied pages inside. Use it to highlight information on award-winning authors and illustrators, comparisons of reference sources on the same subjects, special interest bibliographies, and interesting materials from assorted sources. *Book of Lists*, *Peoples Chronology*, and *Who Won What When* are loaded with useful information. The choices are yours. All you have to do is adapt the format and these few suggestions to get the creative juices flowing.

Fig. 8. Free-standing display for open book

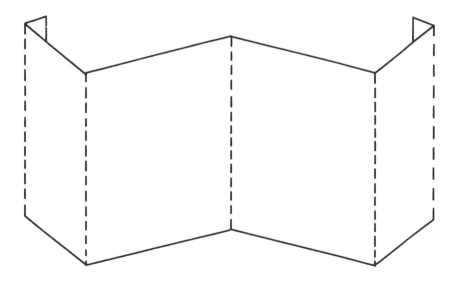

Fig. 9. Open book display

GOOD SUPPLIES TO DISCOVER AND USE

Dietzgen Tape Dots (1-inch dots on a roll) can be pulled off positioned with one hand, which is often desirable when the other hand is needed to hold delicate art elements in place. They're reusable and available at most art supply stores.

Sewing scissors beat any scissors on the market for ease of use and precision, including those specified for artists. You'll find that your hand will fit these scissors better, allowing for more control. Worth the few extra bucks, they'll last forever without resharpening if they are used only for paper.

Blue-line paper is the solution for doing paste-ups for print perfectly straight and in line. These sheets are ruled in grid fashion with nonreproducing blue lines. Sheet sizes, costs, and local dealer information available from Base-Line, Inc., P.O. Box 99068, Seattle, WA 98199.

Nonreproducing blue pencils should be used to rough in measurements, plan spacing, and otherwise provide markings that will not reproduce on finished art for the press. They're available at art supply stores.

Black felt-tip pens for reproduction drawings. Especially recommended is the Esterbrook Rogue 150 pen, because it doesn't have that insipid plastic collar around the tip that the pen companies call an "improvement" (which only cramps your style as you draw). This is another art supply store item.

Light box bargain. If you can't afford a bottom of the line light box (for tracing and paste-up), which costs a minimum of $85, get a slide-sorter viewer box that will fulfill this same function at about half the cost at your photography store.

GOOD ANSWERS TO QUESTIONS
YOU'RE NOT LIKELY TO ASK

Answer: There *is* a source for cartoons about libraries! Al Johns is a professional cartoonist whose work has appeared regularly in *The Saturday Evening Post*. He offers mail-order cartoons on numerous subjects, libraries among them. Cost is $10 a cartoon, with a 25 percent discount if a sheet of eight library cartoons is purchased at one time. Art is ready for reproduction. For information packet write: Cartoons by Johns, Box 1300, Pebble Beach, CA 93953.

Answer: Try spraying your sweaty hands with an antiperspirant (stops all wetness) before doing a tedious hands-all-over-the art-surface job. Also work with paper between the skin and the work surface and you'll say goodbye to unsightly oil smudges on your masterpieces.

GOOD ADVICE

Graphic design, or any art form, is simply expressing in your own way what you see, think, and feel. It is nothing more, even to the pro. The difference between a novice and a pro is that the pro has found and developed a style. If the artist (you?) makes art complex (worries about it), then that artist could develop a complex about art. The solution to the problem is to keep an open mind, a free, bold spirit and *simply do the job*!

Carol Bryan and Phil Douglis

A Crash Course in Photography

Why should photography be a major tool for communicating your library to the public? Because there are times when a photo says it best; says it better than well-written copy or enthusiastic conversation or beautiful artwork.

A good photo can record permanently the *truth* of a scene, whereas the human viewer can only glimpse and relinquish, then try to remember as a writer or speaker or artist. Attempts to recapture and explain with words or drawings sometimes pale in comparison to actuality.

So give your mouth and pen a rest when a photo can do most of the work. Reinforce your P.R. efforts with photographs—in patron and staff publications; in promotional brochures and flyers; in displays explaining services, equipment, and programs; and as accompaniment to press releases.

Let pictures do some of the talking. They can add insight, clarify, persuade and convince, sometimes better than you.

WHAT TYPES OF PHOTOS DO PEOPLE ENJOY MOST?

The only category of photo that has fallen into disfavor is cheesecake, which is definitely passe. The public likes pictures that incorporate:

> Children, especially kids involved in news events or in situations that tug at the heart strings.
> Animals

This article is reprinted with permission from the Fall, 1981, issue of the *Library Imagination Paper*. Portions appeared earlier in IABC News.

Fig. 1. Photo by Lisa Kinney for the Albany County Library bond issue, Laramie, Wyoming.

People, particularly ordinary people doing unusual things, and public figures doing things that liken them to the common man or woman.

Humor

Beauty, something of the sunset or lacy tree variety.

WHAT DOES A GREAT PHOTO HAVE?

A photo that is really outstanding always has one or more of the following qualities:

Impact. A photograph that has impact will be defined as appealing, interesting, impressive, or memorable.

Human interest. A picture that invites emotional reaction of any type, but usually positive in nature.

Effective composition. The simplest composition is usually the best. The work of fine painters and photographers will be inspirational. Don't fear being daring and experimental at times, because "safe" composition may also be dull.

Spontaneity. If your subjects are able to forget about the camera aimed at them because you have involved them with each other, your pictures are likely to be more believable. Natural light and unposed shots help, too.

Effective lighting. If possible, have patience. Outdoor shots are best when the sun is low in the early morning and at sunset time. People, buildings, and mountains are more dramatic in low-angle light. Details lost in shadows don't seem to matter when the light itself is beautiful.

Mood. Photos will exude mystery, gaiety, somberness, or any other emotional aspect.

Contrast. Large and small, near and far, old and new, bright and subtle color.

Imagination. Seeing the commonplace in an artistic way. Remember this every time you press the shutter button!

HOW DO YOU TAKE EFFECTIVE PICTURES?

Try shooting action at the midpoint rather than the end, and letting the viewer complete the action.

Use props to set the scene if they will better explain or create a mood.

Use only the focal point so that the subject "hits you between the eyes." (Some pictures have so much going on they could be split into two pictures.)

Add an item easily identified in terms of size to better explain something of indefinite size, such as a toy car and a human hand.

Use people to convey a message or mood through reaction as well as action.

Add people to an inanimate shot to give the picture life.

Take more than one shot—give yourself several choices of a final photo. Film and processing is relatively inexpensive, and you may not get another chance.

Try both horizontal and vertical shots of a picture.

Take the shot at normal, under, and overexposed settings.

TIPS FOR PHOTOGRAPHING PEOPLE

Take alternate shots from above, eye level, below, left side, center, and right side. People with double chins photograph best from above.

Put your subjects at ease—flatter them, build their egos with compliments about what they are wearing or how great they look. Chat with them about their favorite subjects to take their minds off the camera.

Avoid fluorescent light if possible—natural light is best. Don't use a flash if it is not needed.

In group pictures, it is often more effective to have heads at different levels.

PREPARING A FINISHED PHOTO FOR DISPLAY OR PUBLICATION

Cropping tips:

Crop as tightly as possible, while still retaining the impact and integrity of the shot.

Watch the horizon lines and straighten the tilts by cropping.

Head shots that are used for identification purposes should retain hair, chin, ears, etc. Only when the picture is in-

Fig. 2. Photo by Cathy Audley, Tulsa City-County Library, Tulsa, Oklahoma.

tended as a character study should it be cropped more tightly.

Design tips:

When using a photo in a large layout, start with the picture rather than making the picture fit a predesigned space.

Look for pictures of unusual size for impact. For example, one column × 19", or six column × 2".

Resist the urge to inset one picture into another. The design will be more noticed than the content.

Outlining, or "dropping the background away" from people seldom works well. Use this technique only with inanimate objects.

Photographs will usually be more effective and highlighted if they are used in different sizes in page layout.

In a series of pictures (perhaps interview close-ups), keep the heads the same size.

Use the picture large enough to show what is happening.

A common fault: photo-illustrating stories that don't need to be and neglecting to photo-illustrate those that do.

GOOD TASTE, HONESTY, INTEGRITY . . .

No photos that ridicule people or mislead the viewer, please!

Whenever a photo relies on special effects or was doctored in the darkroom, the cutline should explain how it was achieved.

Give a credit line to the photographer.

WHAT ELSE WILL HELP?

Outstanding photography of library activities is offered in a slide show entitled "Something for Everyone" created by the Louisville Free Public Library. The show won a John Cotton Dana Award in 1981.

If the maze of procedures prior to shooting—focus, distance, exposure settings—has frightened you away from becoming a photographer, forget the past—your problem is solved! Try one of the fabulous all-automatic 35mm cameras (prints and slides) that hit the market in 1981. Just aim and shoot. No settings, no changes, no hassle. Several brands are available, similar in capability and price.

THE TRIBUTE PICTURE—GETTING AWAY FROM THE "GRIP AND GRIN" SHOT

Making and printing pictures to offer visual tributes to people for various accomplishments is often a waste of the reader's valuable time and the publication's valuable space. Yet there are times when a ceremonial event, as recognition, can be used to communicate something to the audience via photographs in print. And that something is often the measure of the human spirit—the caring that people feel for others. It is the job of the photographer to seek out and record such evidence rather than unleashing the flash on a "grip and grin" shot. The photographer must communicate the occasion by capturing with the camera the humanity of the person being honored and the feelings of those who are sharing the event with that person.

SHOOTING SPEAKERS: BEYOND THE "TALKING HEAD"

Making pictures of people making speeches is not easy. That is, you want to say something to your readers about the speaker and the content of the speech. Most speaker pictures fail to go beyond the superficial, "talking head" shot.

If all you want is a good portrait of the speaker, why not try shooting it *before* the speech—during the last minute preparations with slides or notes. Or try *after* the speech, when the speaker is talking privately with a few of the audience members. There are many things you can say about your speakers through your photographs. Just remember that in order to communicate in depth, you must do more than show what the speakers look like. You must also say something about them as people, relate them to their audiences, and, if possible, indicate what kind of knowledge they came to dispense.

Joan Erwin and Sue Fontaine

Public Service Announcements

Public Service Announcements are brief spots—from ten to sixty seconds—broadcast on television and radio free of charge. Libraries can get their share of this free air time. Any message broadcast by television or radio will reach a large number of people, many of whom are beyond the reach of the other media of the library's public relations program. Regular attention to the possibilities offered by public service announcements will generate unique results.

At one time the Federal Communication Commission (FCC) required commercial broadcasters to report their public service time (full-length programs and short spots as well) to help guarantee that the public airwaves were being used for the public good, not just for the profit more easily made through entertainment. In early 1981, the federal government dropped this requirement, leaving the quantity and quality of public service time to the discretion of the station operators. It is reassuring that most stations were already providing more than the minimum of the old guidelines. Community announcements have become a standard in broadcast formats, and they will not easily fall by the wayside.

Since public service announcements fulfill unique needs in a total communications program, even the poorest public service time is a good buy. Even at the time of its smallest listenership, a radio station reaches more library nonusers than the library ever can. Our challenge is to learn how to use this broadcast time skillfully (not a difficult task) and then to routinize the procedures so they are consistently used with a minimum of effort and expense.

To get public service announcements aired around high listenership programs requires imagination, time, and effort. Libraries are competing with national not-for-profit organizations that produce highly professional, appealing announcements to distribute coast to coast. The person who determines which announcements will be aired (perhaps the public service director, community affairs director, the traffic or continuity director, the disc jockey) will attempt to give each organization its "fair share." But as the demand for this free airtime increases, the spots that win out are those that look or sound the best—that is, those having good technical quality and an interesting message; appeal the most to the public service director; or best fit the format of the station. For the latter reason, national producers may deliver the same jingle in rock, country western, or middle-of-the-road style, so that a station may choose the one that best fits its broadcast "personality."

WHEN AND HOW TO USE PUBLIC SERVICE ANNOUNCEMENTS

Public service announcements can be used to publicize an event, to announce a new service, or to remind potential users of a continuing library service. They should be used for information that could be repeated on the air several times a day over a period of a few weeks. They should not be confused with news items, such as the appointment of a new director or the delivery of your 10,000th library card.

Many items of interest, however, would fit both a news format and a public service announcement. When you launch a new service, you might want to write a news release giving all the details, as well as a short announcement to encourage people to take advantage of the new offering. The news release would go to the news director of the broadcast stations (as well as the print media) while the announcement should go to the stations' public service directors. Don't expect the news department to share its release with the person who coordinates the public service announcements. It probably won't happen.

Pay close attention to the important difference in writing radio or television announcements. With television, you have the picture to help convey your meaning, so you can include considerably more information (visually and verbally) than on radio. Because radio messages have to rely completely on the words *as they are heard*, the vocabulary chosen must be easily understood by the listener. For that reason, the announcer speaks more slowly on a radio spot. On radio, you might choose to say almost the same thing in two different ways within a single spot, in order to guarantee that the listener grasps that point. On television, you can use the picture to reinforce a point, and so verbal repetition may not be needed.

HOW TO GET STARTED IN A SMALL COMMUNITY

Contact your station. You may see your station owner at Kiwanis or at church. You may run into your local disc jockey at the grocery store. Express your interest in putting the library's story on the air. Suggest that the library might also be helpful to the radio station! Make an appointment to further discuss your mutual interests. Send (or bring along) your annual report, your program flyers, your story hour schedule, and some books or magazines that will interest the station personnel.

In a small community, you may know that the station manager likes to fish, that the disc jockey has just become a proud father. The more you know about the station and the more you personalize your visit, the more profitable your visit will be. Perhaps a Friend of the Library or a family member can "monitor" your local station(s) for you and give you some comments and ideas before you make your first contact.

Analyze your audience. Even though you are not paying for airtime, you want your library message to produce a positive response. Your station manager or public service director can supply you with statistics on listenership and give you information that will help you develop copy and program themes relevant to the audiences who are listening at specific hours of the day.

Know your local stations. A radio station programs the way it does because it knows something about the community and the people in it. The audience that the library message will reach has already been defined for you by the station. You can identify the age group, and to a good extent, the nature of your listenership by the station format: rock stations gear to young adults; classical music FM stations appeal to educated adults; talk stations attract issue-oriented individuals and "vocal" groups; country western stations have had an increasingly broad appeal to all age groups and all types of people. Keep tabs on the new AM stero stations. More and more of the nation's nearly 5,000 radio stations are attempting to win back audiences from the FM stations. You may find new program opportunities—and new listeners—in this trend that could change listening habits and marketing strategies.

Ask the right questions. For public service spots, you need to know:

Who handles them (sometimes, on a small radio station, it's the disc jockey).

What length does the station accept: ten-, twenty-, thirty-, sixty-second spots?

What length does it air most frequently? If ten-second spots are aired most often, work at telling a ten-second story!

How far in advance does the station need copy? How often should it be changed?

How should the information be presented? The facts (who, what, where, when, how) on a postcard? A complete announcement, accurately timed, that the announcer can read verbatim?

Will the station air "production spots," those with voices that are not those of station personnel; with music, special effects, etc.?

What format does the station require for spots (or for programs): cassettes? reel-to-reel tape? Is it equipped to play recordings? If so, at what speed?

Is the station interested in helping you produce spots? Would it provide you with a sound-proof booth or studio free of charge? Would your local announcer voice the series at no charge? Does the station have copyright-free music and sound effects that you might use?

What recommendations does your station have for making the most of public service airtime? Ask their advice!

Ask what the library can do for the radio station. This is a key point in establishing good working relationships with all media. Media personnel may be totally unaware of the useful professional material that the library holds for them. You can also win good will by calling attention to library materials that meet their personal and family interests. Is your newscaster aware that you have dictionaries that will help him or her pronounce those mystifying foreign names? Atlases that will give the location of little-known cities and provinces? A telephone reference service that will provide needed information quickly, just before he or she goes on the air? Does your favorite disc jockey know that you can supply the biographies of popular artists? Directories of home and business addresses? Does he or she know that you have books of humor and "jokes for all occasions" on your library shelves? Your station manager may be appreciative of current business information, or the latest book on telecommunications. Think not only of what the radio station can do for you, but of what you can do for it. A lively program that attracts new listeners to the station and new users to the library is, of course, the perfect reciprocal relationship.

HOW TO GET STARTED
IN A LARGE MARKET

If the library is in a metropolitan area with a number of radio stations that may serve other library system service areas as well as your own, getting your show on the road may take a little more time. The procedures are similar to those described for smaller communities, but information gathering may be more complicated.

Check your community information sources for a good media list. These are frequently published by government public information officers, by the local Women in Communications chapters, etc. If a local media directory exists, check to see how recently it was published and when the next publication date will be. There is frequent turnover among radio station personnel and any directory over six months old will need updating for names, and possibly for station format. A good directory will provide the names of the station's administrative personnel, including those of the public service director, news director and assignment editor or manager and the program director. You also want the station's address, with zip code, the telephone numbers of each of the above departments, the station's call letters and number on the dial, and for radio, its current format (middle-of-the-road, rock, country, etc.).

Design a file card on which you can record information for each station. The information found by "asking the right questions" can be placed on the other side of the card. Printing a batch of these record cards (and similar ones for television and newspaper contacts) will help assure that you get complete information on your initial calls and will provide a supply for future updating efforts. Checks should be scheduled on a regular basis—every six months is best in a large market, but at least once a year is a "must" unless you can depend upon a media directory to supply correct, current information. Ideally, the library's public relation officer or a P.R. staff member will do the telephoning, because personal contacts should be established. Cooperation and rapport can develop because the public relations officer "speaks the language," has creative ideas for programming, and is prepared to grab opportunities. If staff time is limited, ask a Friend of the Library or a volunteer to telephone each station for the information. This is especially interesting work for a shut-in or a young parent who wants to give community service while the children are napping. The file cards help volunteers do a good job.

And if the reference staff or community information staff at your library ever have lulls in the day's occupation, updating media files is a great way for them to contribute to the library's P.R. program.

PREPARING PUBLIC SERVICE ANNOUNCEMENTS
Finding and Using Ready-made Spots
It is wise to take advantage of high-quality generic radio and television spots that have been produced by other libraries or library associations. Good prerecorded public service announcements can be expensive to produce on your own, so smart library promoters look for ways to share their productions. If you like the mood of the spot and it promotes something your library provides, it is worth considering.

For the last few years, the American Library Association has included good radio spots in its National Library Week promotion package. Because they don't mention National Library Week, these announcements are good for an unlimited length of time. With the support of the Chief Officers of State Library Agencies (COSLA), the 1981 ALA offering featured Bob Newhart in droll skits inviting folks to "call the library." Posters and a marketing kit were available to help local libraries maximize the impact of the campaign. Similar materials are produced each year by the ALA Public Information Office (PIO).

PIO can also put the library in touch with other libraries which have produced successful radio (and television) spots and programs. Like ALA-produced material, some of these can be purchased at low cost. Select the public service spots of your choice and ask the person in charge of public service time at your local radio station to listen to them. If you decide to produce your own materials, listening to public service announcements and programs from other libraries and from PIO will be useful.

State and regional library associations find announcements and promotion kits a good service for their members. Because these have to be general enough to be used by most of their members, they are often usable across the country. Humorous and good examples are the efforts of the Texas Library Association (8989 Westhiemer, Suite 108, Houston, TX 77063) and the Mideastern Michigan Library Cooperative (1026 E. Kearsley Street, Flint, MI 48502). You usually hear about these through library-related publications or see them at the "P.R. Swap 'n' Shop" or the John Cotton Dana audiovisual presentation sponsored by the Public Relations Section of the Library Administration and Management Association at ALA annual conferences.

Often these "canned" spots will leave a few seconds free at the end for you to enter a local tag, your own identification. Broadcaster often want a local feeling in their spots to increase listener appeal. A cooperative station can add this tag for you. You might be able to get one television station to make "dubs" (duplicate videotapes) of the spots for all the other stations in town. This kind of cooperation with nonprofit organizations is not unusual.

You will need to purchase at least one copy of the prerecorded spot from the original producer; they usually don't mind if you have dubs made for each local station. In 1981, the cost of a set of one or more radio spots averaged between $5 and $15, and television spots were around $50. (Because of the COSLA support, the Bob Newhart spots were provided to libraries in many cooperating states at no charge.) These are incredible bargains, given the amount of talent and effort that goes into a good production.

Writing Original Announcements
Each announcement should be carefully constructed for two reasons. First, you have a very short amount of time to communicate your whole message. Second, the individuals in the audience don't usually concentrate on the content of commercials or public service announcements. The message must be clear and concise.

140

"Talk terse." Choose short words. Use simple sentences.

Vary the pace: a short sentence, then a longer sentence. In a script, use dots . . . to indicate verbal pauses.

Use action words. Give the listener something to do: attend a program, visit the library, check out a book, etc.

Use descriptive, colorful words to create visual images.

Avoid putting a key point (such as the date of a program) in the opening words of your message. It takes a second or two for listeners to tune in to a short announcement and they can easily miss the first few syllables.

Read your announcements out loud to see if they read smoothly. Don't write "tongue twisters."

Read your copy aloud to *another* person to see if your message is easily understood.

Be lively and imaginative, but don't be "cute." When in doubt be straightforward, tell the "5 Ws" (who, what, why, when, where). You may also have time for "how."

Time your spots. A 10-second announcement is about 25 words; a 20-second announcement is about 50 words; a 60-second announcement is about 150 words.

Type your spot announcements (and news copy, etc.) double spaced.

Include your name and telephone number (including your home phone number if you aim for night programming).

At the top of the page, state the date that you want the announcement to *begin to air* and *when they should stop.*

Supply the station(s) with *general* spots that can run *any* time. Update these from time to time.

Remember to thank your station occasionally for the public service (and other airtime) that they have given to you.

Visualizing for Television

Television public service announcements have the added advantage of a visual component that can add to the effectiveness of your message. There is also the danger that the visual part can detract from your message, if the picture does not relate closely to the sound track.

There are several ways to get a public service announcement on television. You can send the station the same copy you send to the radio station, and let the station supply the visual. They might run your announcement over a slide that reads "Community Bulletin Board" or "Blanktown Public Library Presents" or "Channel 7 Salutes." This is easy to do on a continuing basis, sending a new announcement at least every month or so.

If you can provide a *good* 35mm slide of your library or someone using the particular service you're promoting, that's even better. A good slide means one with good color and an adequate wide border within the picture part of the slide that can be lost without losing the essential part of the photo. The TV camera and broadcast system cuts off at least fifteen percent of the side margins and five percent of the top and bottom margins of the picture, so the "critical area" of your shot should be well within the center of the part that will be chopped off.

Because a television screen is wider than it is tall (in an approximate ratio of four units wide to three units tall), a slide must be shot with a horizontal format. A vertical slide would leave a wide black band on each side of the screen. The same three-by-four ratio is the appropriate format for an "art card" that you might provide for the station to use to make a slide. An artist makes an art card by putting a drawing or color photo and very few words on a sturdy, brightly colored background with wide margins all around the "critical area" that you want to show on the television screen. Then the station can make a slide of the art card, perhaps after adding its own channel number in one corner, or the station can put the art card on videotape with your narration in the background. (See figure 1.)

PREPARING ARTWORK FOR TELEVISION SLIDES

Prepare art on an 11" × 14" card. On a tissue overlay, center a 6" × 8" window. This is the frame to align with the outside edges of your 35mm camera viewfinder when shooting. Still working on the tissue, center a 4" × 6" image area within the 6" × 8" window.

Keep all artwork well within the 4" × 6" image area. Do not place critical information in the corner areas. Illustrations or photos can bleed off edges if desired.

Remember that art must be readable in both color and black and white. Stick to strong contrasting colors such as yellow on dark blue or white on any dark color.

When ready to shoot, use the 6" × 8" frame on the tissue as a framing guide. Then lift the tissue and shoot.

If the 4" × 6" image area is not large enough for your particular artwork, enlarge all dimensions proportionately. For

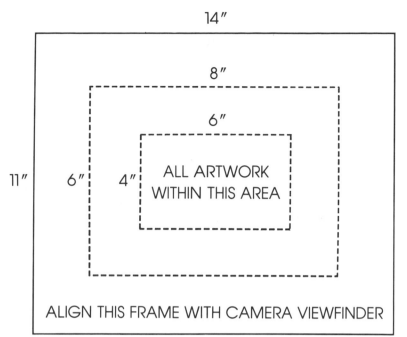

14"

8"

6"

11"   6"   4"   ALL ARTWORK
WITHIN THIS AREA

ALIGN THIS FRAME WITH CAMERA VIEWFINDER

Fig. 1. Art card for television slide

example, use a 22″ × 28″ card with a 12″ × 16″ frame and a 9″ × 12″ image area.

Simplicity is a plus with TV visuals. A close-up of one librarian and one child is better than a storyteller swamped with children. An art card with just two or three words is much more effective than one with eight.

Sometimes a station will offer to produce film or videotape public service announcements for the library. This is a bonus in more than one way. When a station has been involved in producing it, the announcement has a better chance of getting a lot of airtime instead of sitting unshown on the shelf. To secure this kind of cooperation, draft three or four possible spots and take the scripts to the station's public service director. It's usually a good idea to focus on one particular service you'd like promoted in each spot, rather than to try to tell the whole library story in just thirty seconds. But if you're drafting three or four spots from which a producer can choose, it doesn't hurt to include one that's a potpourri of the wonders of the library. In this kind of multipurpose spot, it is particularly important that the picture being seen closely matches the words being heard. Otherwise the confusion between the eye and ear creates such a jumble that no message will reach the brain.

BUYING AIR TIME

Someday you'll have a grant that gives you much more flexibility and a better budget than you've ever had for a public relations campaign. The temptation might be to spend some of that money on air time to guarantee that your spots get played often and at the right times of day. Paying for broadcast time or print advertising space is almost always a bad idea. Unless you spread your dollars fairly among all the media (broadcast, print, billboards, etc.), you'll offend the ones that are left out to the point that they might refuse to give you the free public service space you've come to expect. Competition among commercial advertisers is serious business, and libraries should beware of crossing that line. The main exception to this rule is in a bond issue referendum or other voter-oriented campaign, which by law are not entitled to public service donations. On these political promotions, you can try to get free news space but you may not accept free advertising or spot announcement donations without reporting them as political contributions.

However, some libraries, particularly those in smaller settings, have reported that they have been successful in achieving library communications goals by purchasing radio spots. One librarian in New York State noted that their local station gave several free spots for every spot purchased, so that they not only got better placement, but more than doubled their coverage. In considering paid announcements, here are some questions to ask: May we spend tax dollars for advertisement? Perhaps the Friends of the Library can purchase spots. Perhaps a corporation or business firm will sponsor a program (Chesebrough-Pond's in Greenwich, Connecticut, for years sponsored a fifteen-minute radio program for the library with only a credit line). Perhaps the library can even "trade out" with the station just as many airlines, etc., "trade out" broadcast promotions. Will we incur the ill will of other media if we choose one station on which to spend limited funds (obviously one would choose the station with the highest audience rating or the best target audience for the library's message)? Will we lose our public service or "nonprofit" image, and thus lose out on "free" coverage? Will it be appropriate "politically" and in regard to public relations?

Professional P.R. practitioners remind us that publicity is only a tool in a long-range program. Don't depend on it to do your whole job—but do depend upon it to accomplish the job it does best—reaching a mass market, getting messages out directly and quickly to targeted audiences.

And remember the fourth step in the P.R. process—evaluation. Compare the number of news releases, public service announcements, etc. that you send out with the number printed and aired. Was your time spent productively? Check occasionally to learn how your users learned of a service or a program. The use of simple surveys will help identify which media are the most effective for you. Spend some time in analyzing how much time you are spending on various news and public service activities. Is the effort expended to prepare a fifteen-minute story hour broadcast time well spent, or would it be better to work on spot announcements across a range of subjects?

If you are in a large market, you have to share radio and television public service time not only with other nonprofit organizations, but with other libraries. Join together to produce quality spots and programs that benefit everyone. "Use Your Library," "Your Information Place—The Library," "Check Out Your Library" are among the general themes and slogans that can work for all of you.

Radio and television are "hot" media. Take a look at your local programming; take a listen to your station formats. Tune in. Tie in. You may find that for your library, radio and television are red hot!

BRIEF BIBLIOGRAPHY

Broadcast Publicity. One of a series originally prepared by the Leaflets Com. and revised by the Publications Com., Public Relations Sect., Library Administration Div., American Library Assn., 50 E. Huron St., Chicago, IL 60611.
If You Want Airtime: A Handbook for Publicity Chairmen. National Assn. of Broadcasters. 1771 N St. N.W., Washington DC 20036.
Mass Media Marketing of Library Services or How to Win in the Competition for Public Service Advertising Time on Radio and Television. Peggy Barber, dir., Public Information Office, American Library Assn., 50 E. Huron St., Chicago, IL 60611.
PRepare: The Library Public Relations Recipe Book. Irene Moran, ed. Public Relations Sect., Library Administration Div., American Library Assn., 50 E. Huron St., Chicago, IL 60611. 1978. "PSA Writing," p. 19, by Rita Kohn.

Peggy Howe and Sue Fontaine

News Releases

First of all, what is "news?" News, according to Charles A. Dana, editor of the old *New York Sun*, is "anything that will make people talk." And Turner Catledge, a former managing editor of the *New York Times*, called news "anything you can find out today that you didn't know before." For our purposes, news is also what can be printed, and so our news should be in the best and most usable form. Thus, releases must be something that readers didn't know yesterday.

HARD NEWS AND FEATURE STORIES

Hard news covers a wide variety of events, from floods and fires to significant speeches, conferences, and controversies. Alerting a reporter in advance of an event will help to get coverage, and a follow-up phone call can be helpful.

Features are loosely defined as personality or organizational profiles or background material that goes beyond the immediate headlines to explore how the situation came about, what is being done about it, and what's expected to happen next. An interview with a library board chairman or director would usually be called a feature.

The difference is a little fuzzy, but hard news is always timely, referring mainly to current events. Features are less so, and some can be printed anytime. Some features do have deadlines, as, for instance, features on National Library Week or National Children's Book Week (what we're doing for observance). You may suggest features to your newspaper reporter, either in person, by mail, or by telephone.

HOW TO WRITE THE NEWS

A well-written news story saves the reporter's precious time. All other things being equal, a reporter nearing a deadline with a choice between two stories will print the one that's better written. This means that the person in charge of your news releases must be familiar with some basic news writing techniques.

Most newspapers use what's called "AP (for Associated Press) Style" for dealing with capitalization, punctuation, and abbreviations. This style book is available from the Associated Press. However, observing a few other basic guidelines will make your release more likely to be among those in the coveted "printed" category, instead of the round file. In newspaper offices this "round file" is of giant size, and good stories in unusable forms regularly become part of its contents.

First of all, use your own letterhead or news release stationery. Always triple or double space.

On page one, include the name, address, and telephone number of your library, a name and (working hours) telephone number of contact person (if different from the library's number), and release date. For example: "For release: immediately" (which is whenever they receive it) or "For release: after noon, Saturday, June 1, and thereafter."

Always type on only one side of the page. Newspaper people are not accustomed to looking on the back side. If your story is longer than one page, type "more" at the bottom. Across the top of page two, type the page number, subject, date, library's name, and the name and telephone number of the contact person. For example: "Page 2—Pet Show—July 25, 1980—Anytown Public Library—Joe Doe—Telephone (555) 555–5722."

The news story is written in inverted pyramid style. Newspapers work with limited space that is further diminishing daily as newsprint prices increase and conservation measures are applied. You've also heard that the *New York Times* promises "all the news that's fit to print?" Well, newspapers actually print all the news that fits. So, when a story is too long it is chopped off, literally, from the bottom because nobody has time to rewrite it. As a consequence, whatever wasn't said above the cropping doesn't get printed. Therefore, all the information should appear in the first two or three paragraphs—all five Ws (who, what, where, when, why) and the H (how). After that, further details are arranged in descending order of importance:

the most important facts coming right after the lead paragraph and the least important further down in the story.

A good catchy lead will sometimes pique the interest of the news editor and your story will make it when another, duller one, won't. Be concise. Space is at a premium. Use adjectives: "New York's Bellevue Hospital" instead of "Bellevue Hospital in New York." Don't use jargon familiar only to librarians (not "SOLINET" but "Southeastern Library Network"). Identify everybody and everything in the first mention, for instance, "President Ronald Reagan"; thereafter just "Reagan" or "President Reagan."

Always use the full date, for example, "June 12," not "next Thursday." Sometimes, however, in your lead sentence you may say, "A pet show will be the highlight of next week's children's library program. On Sunday, May 12, children of all ages will bring their pets. . . ." But be sure to include the date somewhere *very* near the top of your story. Provide the time of day and whether A.M. or P.M. "At the 8 P.M. ceremonies, Dr. Smith was installed as the new board chairman."

Use full street numbers of buildings even if they are well known.

It's useful to attach a copy of a program or agenda. Include in your story the purpose of an event and information about where to get tickets.

Make it local! Some editors *promise* they won't use *anything* that isn't local. These usually are editors of nondailies with strong competition from nearby large dailies. For guidance, study your local paper.

Provide complete information. Newspaper reporters have a high turnover rate—their assignments are switched. "Your" reporter last month may have been promoted or moved on to a larger city, and the new one may not know you've just moved into the new building.

Do not editorialize (the art exhibit you're opening may be "beautiful" to you but not to someone else).

Double check every spelling, especially names. Use complete names, including middle initial. Do not use abbreviations (does "assoc." mean "associations" or "associates"?). Use full name at first mention, then initials or acronyms (American Library Association, then ALA).

Where possible, use a quote. Be sure the statement is newsworthy. Have the director or board chairman tell how the grant will be used to aid the community. "Gratitude for grant" is not news.

Provide identifying information. For instance, "American Library Association, national organization of librarians."

Always finish the sentence on one page; in other words, don't begin a sentence on page one and end it on page two. Sometimes different people get pages of a story to be typeset.

Remember, use short paragraphs. Two or three sentences are sufficient.

Type releases individually and duplicate mechanically. Do not use carbon copies. All recipients should get identical material, not originals here, copies there.

PHOTOS

Photographs should be of people in action, unposed, sharp and clear. Polaroids don't reproduce well; 8″ × 10″ glossies are preferred. Do not send color unless by previous arrangement. "Action" is not Mr. Smith presenting a check to the director. Action is the architect with the director looking over plans for the new library building or the children's librarian setting up facilities for the upcoming story hour.

In the case of news about a person, such as "John Jones is appointed director," supply a reproducible, black-and-white portrait (mug shot). For a group photo, three people are best, five, the absolute maximum. Remember, photos of children are popular with editors.

If you have old photographs, you may ask if your reporter would be interested. Sometimes a clear photograph taken in 1880 of a library building has as much or more appeal than a recent shot. If so, arrange to have the old photo copied. Never send your original.

With any picture, provide a descriptive caption (cutline), typed on white paper and attached at the bottom of the photo and folded over the face of the photo. Two or three sentences should be adequate for the cutline. Identify persons, places and things, and point the reader's attention to areas of special interest (for processing and printing, the photograph will be separated from the typewritten news story). You may telephone the reporter to make sure the prints were received in satisfactory condition.

Always try to send photographs you do *not* want returned. It is difficult for the copy desk to keep track of and return material.

GETTING YOUR NEWS IN PRINT

After your excellent news story is written, what then? Obviously it needs to be in the hands of the local newspaper. To do this there are several things you need to know, and among the first is "your" reporter—the person whose assignment includes your library.

Designate one person in your library to be the official information officer and have that person talk to the reporter frequently. Avoid the title "publicity chairman." Newspapers are in the business of informing, not publicizing.

Your news is best in writing. However, you may always call your reporter, too, telling of interesting events to come—anything of potential interest to many people—such as photo possibilities; shows, special programs, exhibits, musical performances, new books or collections ("library adds business collection"), special grants, new equipment (teletypewriter for deaf, toys for kids, paintings to lend), library staff awards and achievements, scholarships, newly elected officers, staff promotions, honors, etc.

Provide information regularly, but not with the attitude "It's Monday—time to do a news release." Have a reason to send a release.

Address the envelope to your assigned reporter, if you have one. If not, send releases to the appropriate news desk. Spell the name of the reporter accurately on the envelope. Misspelling indicates the sender is not a regular reader. Very bad. Worse still: try *not* to send to a predecessor! Newspapers have heavy turnover.

It is a good idea for you to follow up with a phone call, after your release is mailed, to see if the reporter received your release or needs more information.

If your reporter calls after he or she receives your release, be sure you're fully armed with facts. If you do not know the answer to a question, get it quickly—as soon as possible—and report back immediately. Remember the reporter's ever-present deadlines. He or she may have been given only a few minutes to write your story and at the last moment discovers a vital fact has been omitted; you will need to know the answer or find it quickly. Here we're often talking about minutes before the deadline. And, of course, if the reporter doesn't get the fact at that last minute, the space for your story just may be filled with another organization's news.

And above all, be truthful! This cannot be emphasized enough. Don't try to cover up embarrassment—you lose credibility. It may take years to recover. The memory of your deception can outlast any good your organization can do.

Give the story first to the newspaper before advertising anywhere else. Otherwise it's not news. If there are two papers in town, give both a chance for a scoop alternately or release to both at the same time.

After your release appears, remember to thank your reporter.

TIMING

Deadlines, of course, are among a newspaper's greatest concerns. For nondailies, the deadlines vary according to the day of publication, but are no less urgent or exacting. A small weekly may hire only two or three staff members—very busy people!

How far in advance should you send your material? Nondailies can give you a definite deadline for news to appear in the next issue. Dailies are not as easy to schedule. Their deadlines vary depending on the day of the week. Sunday is perhaps the best-read edition. Most Sunday papers have a Tuesday or Wednesday deadline. Be aware of the deadlines for all issues of your newspaper.

Mondays are usually good days for your release to appear, since Mondays are sometimes slow newsdays. Wednesdays or Thursdays often contain grocery ads, producing larger papers, hence more room for your release. Become informed about the schedules your newspapers follow, the format they use, and the sections that appear regularly in each issue.

Check deadlines. Almost 100 percent of the time reporters want to know *before* something happens, not *after*. To a reporter, stale news is no news. Consider your lead time. Remember, if you mail your release today, the soonest it can reach the newspaper is tomorrow, and that makes it the next day before it can possibly be published.

Ask questions. Arrange to discuss your library when your reporter is not under deadline pressure. Ask the reporter for the newspaper's policies, procedures, and deadlines. Ask the reporter's advice. For example, some newspapers print lists of new books at the library; others don't. So don't waste your time and your library's credibility by sending what they don't want; you are only demonstrating to one and all that you're not familiar with their newspaper.

Furnish your reporter with a fact sheet about the library with its name, address, and names and addresses of board members and director for handy reference.

Other questions will arise in your mind from time to time; for answers, ask your reporter.

NEWS RELEASES FOR TELEVISION AND RADIO

Getting television and radio coverage of library news is a slightly different matter from getting newspaper coverage. Here are a few tips. For other hints on developing relationships with broadcast media, see the selection on public service announcements.

Get to know the newscasters and news formats of the various local stations.

Get acquainted with the news director, news assignment director, etc., of each station.

Find out if the station takes news over the telephone in the form of reports or interviews taped by phone and aired later.

Compile a list of library persons who make good reporters or interviewees, such as trustees, staff members, or Friends of the Library.

Write special news releases for radio and television. Radio and television style differs from newspaper style by being generally briefer and more colorful. Broadcast news releases should, however, be delivered in the same way as other news releases: to the correct person, with full address, name of library contact person, etc. If you simply can't supply specially written releases, let the stations know that you can't but that you hope they can draw from your "all media" news copy. They may, or may not, have time to rewrite.

Do not supply as news that which should be presented as a public service announcement. Unless there is something new or unusual about your library services, your information has a better chance of being publicized in another format. However, if you're establishing a new service, have amazing statistics on use, are doing a library survey, or have an outstanding program speaker or a unique program, consider it news, call your news directors, and let the stations decide. You may be happily surprised to find yourself on the 6 o'clock news.

Keep in mind the value of broadcast media for emergency information. Only by television and radio, for example, can you let the community know the library is closed because of snow.

If these seem to be a lot of guidelines, remember most are just common sense; they will become routine in a short time. And after that—happy publicity!

Alice Norton

What Every Library Needs
(and Why)—An Annual Report

Every library should produce and energetically distribute an annual report. The annual report communicates the whole library story to those who may be aware of only one or two aspects of the library's operations. A report can also demonstrate that the library is a well-managed agency with administrators who are in touch with their publics and skillful in both securing and using resources. The content of the report and the medium that the library uses to communicate both project the library's message and its image as an institution.

AUDIENCES

Insiders

The first step in planning any form of communication is to identify the persons and groups to whom the message is directed. Before the library administration communicates with others, administrators should share the news with library staff, including any volunteer workers. Every library staff member should know and understand the report's message (and, ideally, should have contributed to it). It damages a library's reputation and weakens the self-esteem of staff when outsiders know more about the library's operations than those who work there.

Library Decision Makers

A primary audience for the report is the group of persons who both determine and influence the library's policy and budget. Some of these persons are close at hand, such as public library trustees, school principals, academic library committees, members and corporate executives. Others are more remote persons,

154

such as elected and appointed government officials, college trustees and alumni, and company stockholders.

Library Users

Most persons who use a library are aware primarily of those services that relate to their needs and interests. In planning an annual report, it is useful to divide the library users into sub-groups according to the services the library supplies them with, the ways they secure services (visits, phone, mail), and the most effective ways to communicate with them. Potential library users from the same groups are also important target markets. A library annual report can stimulate more use as well as report on services and operations.

Other Agencies

Every organization with which a library has dealings is a potential annual report audience. And for every type of library, the categories are different. Examples are: other libraries, community organizations, educational agencies, associations, business firms, and suppliers of materials and services.

Communicators

For annual report planners, key persons whose job is communication may range from a reporter or editorial writer on a daily newspaper or a television newscaster to the editor of a school or company newsletter. These persons can use the annual report message in two ways—as background for their year-round communication about the library and as a news story.

MESSAGES

Resources and Services

Although an annual report focuses on a specific time period, it doesn't *have* to be titled "annual report." For many persons these words carry dreary connotations. In addition to covering events of one time period, the report should also present a vivid, accurate picture of the library's current resources and services. To evaluate whether the report does this, the report producer should test it with newcomers who have little prior knowledge of the library.

The report should present significant events of the time period covered with appealing human interest examples and anecdotes and financial figures for income (including sources) and expenditures. The library's purpose should be either explicitly stated or implied, and the report should include the legal or political base (to tell who's ultimately in charge). Statistics should be meaningful—neither too many (which overwhelm) nor too few (such as figures used without those from an earlier year for comparison).

Interpretation

Every report needs a theme to capture attention, cement the various parts together, and present its central message. This message should be so carefully defined that it could be stated in one sentence. For example, one public library used as a report theme: "The Ferguson Library is good—but not good enough." Everything in the brief leaflet supported this statement, both by presenting resources and services with their benefits to the community and also by showing weaknesses in resources and gaps in services. It is useful to follow the identification of a library's needs with a recommendation for meeting them. (How much money, how many staff, what resources or physical facilities are necessary to bring the library up to a standard of excellence?)

Some skilled administrators interpret their institution's services and actions against a background of what is happening outside—in terms of the economy, of political change, or of technological advances and opportunities. Frank statements of shortcomings and problems may attract support for solving them. Candid reporting will also increase the library's reputation for credibility and will give authority to the library administrator's recommendations for improvement.

Facts

Perhaps less important than the message, but still essential, are such facts as these: the library's name, address (including state), telephone number, date of publication, and usually the names of key staff and decision makers such as trustees or advisory committees.

PRODUCTION AND DISTRIBUTION

Form

Some readers of this article will probably have noticed that the discussion of audiences and content omit mention of the form of the report. A printed annual report, produced in many copies and distributed in person or by mail is the most usual form, both for libraries and for other agencies. The annual report planner, however, should consider every possible medium (or a combination of them) before making a final decision. An elementary school media center might decide on a bookmark prepared, illustrated, and produced by students. A small library might communicate through a movable display, shown first in the library and then at banks, community centers, and meeting rooms throughout the village. A college library might call on the resources of the campus film department to produce a videotape report for airing on television and in the library on small videoplayers. A newspaper feature article with photographs could do triple duty, first in the newspaper, then blown up for poster exhibits, and finally as inexpensive reprints used as handouts and direct mail pieces.

The questions to ask before selecting the form should be: Which media will most effectively carry the message to the major audiences? Which media can the library economically use (keep in mind that staff time also has a dollar value) to produce a report of appropriate quality?

SUGGESTIONS FOR SUCCESS

The library administrator should assign the major responsibility for the report to one person and identify the roles others will play. Staff are indispensable in supplying examples of library use to humanize the report and in making suggestions about content and format. If everyone on the staff, however, feels he or she has the last word on either, the report will be delayed and may even be canceled.

The person in charge of the report should start work early. When evaluating the current year's report, initial plans for next year's report should begin.

The library should seek the widest possible distribution of its message. It adds relatively little to the overall cost to produce extra copies of a printed report or make additional copies of a cassette. The report should always be available for newcomers to the library, whether its form is a printed leaflet the new user gets with a borrower's card on an initial visit or an exhibit or slide/sound show he or she is invited to see.

Other opportunities are contests, such as those the Library Public Relations Council sponsors, and the public relations

157

swap-'n'-shop sessions that the American Library Association's Public Relations Section and other associations sponsor at annual conferences. If mailing costs in filling requests present a problem, the library can offer to mail a free copy in exchange for an addressed envelope or label and postage. A report in the form of a poster, with an appealing design and a compelling slogan, may be marketed for sale. Sometimes a bank or store will enclose a small library report in its regular mailing to customers. The library can offer copies of the report at meetings and other gatherings of the library's target audiences.

For administrators of some libraries, issuing an annual report is a legal requirement or an executive order. Staff of every library, however, should view the annual report as an opportunity to catch the attention of important publics, communicate facts and interpretations to them and then motivate these groups to action.

HOW EIGHT LIBRARIES REPORTED

The Tulsa City-County Library in Oklahoma used in an eight-page section in *TV World*, a magazine supplement to the *Tulsa Daily World*. Human interest pictures with captions used the style of a department store catalog to present the library's services. The supplement also included a map of library locations, a phone directory, library hours, and information on how to get a library card and join the Friends. Funds for the supplement and 15,000 reprints for use all year came from corporations.

The Newport Public Library in Rhode Island translated its official annual report to government officials into a daily newspaper feature for the library's regular column, "The Grist Mill." The library made reprints for its own distribution and for a wide mailing by the Friends of the Library.

The year after the University of Connecticut library moved to a new building, the annual report for the entire university included a major section on the library. The report identified the move as a "significant event of the year" and included many photographs of the new facility.

The Foundation Center in New York City offered its annual report both as a printed pamphlet and on microfiche.

The Oklahoma Department of Libraries reported about the preceding calendar year in the first six pages of the January issue of *ODL Source*, an eight-page monthly newsletter. Included were highlights of the year, a financial chart, departmental reports, and staff pictures. The newsletter also carried three sections not in the report: announcements of new publications, staff appointments, and continuing education opportunities. The library produced 3,000 copies of the newsletter that had space for a bulk mailing address.

The New Jersey State Library issued a special summer edition of its newsletter, *Impressions*, for a capsule version of five years of library actions during a time of change. Written in diary form, the report included a one-page article, "Looking Ahead . . ." by the state librarian.

The National Library of Medicine told readers of *National Library of Medicine News* about notable events of the previous year on page one in a letter from the director.

The Evansville (Indiana) Public Library and Vanderburgh County Public Library used one side of a plastic book bag to answer the question "Did you know?" with facts about library operations and a report on the preceding year.

Part Four

Some
Special Resources

Kathleen Kelly Rummel and Joan Erwin

The American Library Association and Good Public Relations

The American Library Association offers many kinds of support for local public relations efforts. The Library Administration and Management Association (LAMA), a division of ALA, includes a very active Public Relations Section (PRS).

The Public Relations Section offers many programs on public relations at the annual summer ALA conferences. A typical convention program includes a two-and-a-half-day preconference on the nuts and bolts of library public relations, a session on newsletter production, a showing of the best in library audiovisual efforts, and a "swap'n'shop" where you can pick up samples of library promotion pieces from around the country and talk one-to-one with experts in a dozen areas of library promotion. LAMA may soon be offering regional P.R. workshops in cooperation with state library associations, state libraries, or regional library conferences.

LAMA's Public Relations Section also cosponsors, with the H. W. Wilson Company, the John Cotton Dana Awards, which recognize outstanding public relations efforts among libraries in the English-speaking world. ALA's headquarters library collects all the scrapbook presentations of recent Dana Award winners, sources of inspiration, which are available on interlibrary loan. ALA also offers inexpensive pamphlets on the subject of library publicity (prepared by the PRS) and slightly more expensive audiotapes of library conference programs on P.R. topics.

With the advice of the National Library Week Committee, ALA produces excellent National Library Week materials (posters, bookmarks, television and radio spots) that are usable all year around. Sales of these reasonably priced items produce income for ALA's ongoing efforts to increase public awareness of libraries through national media outlets.

Some of the P.R. concerns addressed by the section's programs and projects include the effective interpretation of the library program and profession, relations of the library staff with its clientele, successful use of communications media to provide information about library services and resources, training for library staff in P.R. techniques and communications skills, and fostering the growth of the Friends of the Libraries movement.

Membership in the section is open to all members of the Library Administration and Management Association of the American Library Association. Friends activities are stressed by the section and all friends of libraries—individuals and organizations—are encouraged to join! Its committees include:

Friends, Volunteers, and Advocates Committee. This excellent, active committee was responsible for the organization of the new national group called "Friends of Libraries U.S.A." The move to organize a national Friends group has been underway for many years and, under the chairmanship of Sandy Dolnick, the PRS Friends of the Library Committee was instrumental in seeing that such a group was finally able to organize. This committee now focuses on the needs of library administrators and managers in working with Friends groups and has broadened its charge to include volunteers and advocates.

The John Cotton Dana Public Relations Awards Committee. This committee recommends policies and procedures and serves as jury for the selection of winners of the John Cotton Dana Public Relations Awards. This awards program is jointly sponsored by the H. W. Wilson Company and the Public Relations Section to encourage excellent P.R. programs and campaigns for libraries; it is the most prestigious and most sought after of all library public relations awards.

The Publications Committee. This committee prepares brochures, bibliographies, and other publications and informational materials to assist libraries in developing P.R. and publicity techniques and conducting P.R. programs. The committee is also involved in sponsoring continuing education programs having to do with library publications and supports the work of the other PRS committees as they pertain to publications.

Public Relations Services to Libraries Committee. The busiest of all PRS committees involved with programming, this committee has been the group responsible for most of the section's continuing education activities. The committee is charged with considering library public relations needs and conducting programs and activities to aid librarians and trustees in meeting those needs. The very successful annual "Swap 'n' Shop," the section's preconferences held to train library staffs in P.R. basics and communications techniques, annual ALA Conference programming, and the consideration of public relations needs for all types of libraries are in the bailiwick of this committee. It continues each year to improve upon the activities of the last and is increasingly responsive to the needs of the library public relations community.

Public Relations Services to State Libraries and State Library Associations Committee. This recently established committee is responsible for a wide range of activities. Some of its plans call for the development of a national library Public Information Officer directory on the regional, state, and multistate levels; the development of guidelines for the establishment and operation of a library public information office and activities—again, on the regional, state, and multistate levels; and the planning and presentation of conference and institute P.R. programs directed to the staffs of system, regional, and state libraries and associations. The committee also recently completed a survey of state and regional libraries and associations that requested information about their P.R. programs.

Ad Hoc Institute Planning Committee. The Public Relations Section feels that it is necessary to "take the section to its membership" and this committee was formed to plan, develop, and conduct regional public relations institutes throughout the country throughout the year.

Planning and Priorities Committee. This committee is charged with considering ideas for future PRS projects.

The Public Relations Section is obviously a very busy organization. But its members want to be busier and they must be if the section is to continue to increasingly support the library community's effort to better its public relations. Join the Public

Relations Section! It provides valuable opportunities to learn more about good library public relations and to meet the many others who are concerned about the future of libraries. To join, contact the Library Administration and Management Association, American Library Association, 50 East Huron, Chicago, Illinois 60611.

Peggy Barber

National Library Week –
A Few Words from the Sponsor

It takes a long time for a new thread to become part of the fabric of library administration, but National Library Week has made it. Twenty-eight consecutive years of celebrations have put our special week on most library calendars. To some of our colleagues National Library Week (NLW) is a glorious opportunity; to others it's a big yawn.

We at ALA regularly check the concept for tarnish and reexamine the original enthusiasm. Does the public still take libraries for granted? Do librarians take National Library Week for granted? Who started NLW and why? Does it still work?

ORIGIN OF NATIONAL LIBRARY WEEK

In the mid-1950s American libraries and book publishers were concerned about a drop in personal spending for books that occurred while spending for musical instruments, radios, and television sets increased. The implication was that Americans were reading less. To encourage reading and to keep books widely available, the American Library Association (ALA) and the American Book Publishers Council called together a group of concerned librarians, publishers, teachers, and citizens. Thus, in 1954, the National Book Committee (NBC), a nonprofit citizen's organization, was formed.

NBC's goals were to encourage people to read in their increasing leisure time so as to develop appreciative audiences for the arts, to enlist support for civic betterment, to raise scholarship levels in schools and colleges, to improve incomes and health and to develop strong and happy family life—ambitious goals for a small group committed to books.

In 1957 NBC developed a plan for National Library Week. Individual cities and states had sponsored library weeks in previous years with great success. The Junior Chamber of Commerce of Youngstown, Ohio, originated the observance of Library Week in 1937. Jackson, Mississippi, had celebrated "Know Your Library Week," and California had had several statewide observances.

During the week of March 16–22, 1958, the United States and Canada were advised to "Wake Up and Read!" The week's activities were planned by NBC in cooperation with ALA through local and state committees. The Advertising Council approved NLW as a public service campaign, and President Dwight Eisenhower kicked off the week with a proclamation that called for "the fullest participation" by the people of the United States. More than 5,000 cities and towns joined in the celebration, setting library records in circulation and registration.

In 1959 NLW again was observed, and the ALA Council voted to continue the week annually in April. Canadian libraries and publishers formed the Canadian Library Week Council to celebrate the week at the same time as the United States.

Pitney Bowes created its first postage meter ad for NLW in 1962. In 1969 the United Kingdom asked six American librarians to travel through the United Kingdom during its own third NLW. In 1975 NLW became the occasion for Legislative Day in Washington, D.C. On this day each year during NLW, librarians and trustees personally tell legislators of library needs.

Motivating people to read was the primary purpose of NLW as run by NBC. They reasoned that, once motivated, people would support and use libraries. Most NLW themes focused on reading—"Read—The Fifth Freedom" (1963), "Be All You Can Be—Read" (1968–69), "Get Ahead—Read" (1973).

In 1974 NBC disbanded, and ALA's NLW Committee and Public Information Office continued the tradition of National Library Week. The theme shifted to more direct emphasis on libraries and information services. The 1975 "Information Power" campaign won two top public relations awards. The Public Relations Society of America panel said, "Libraries no longer looked dull, they looked alive and exciting." Recent themes like "Info to Go . . . At the Library" (1978) and "America's Greatest Bargain ... The Library" (1980) have kept libraries spotlighted as a vital national resource.

National Library Week was the first truly national program for library promotion, and in creating it the National Book Committee established a sensible formula for combining national publicity with active local citizen and press involvement. When NLW came to ALA it gave the association a leadership role in an area that had previously been neglected— increasing public awareness of library services. So, in addition to providing materials and ideas for local celebrations of libraries, ALA publicizes National Library Week on network television and radio, through national wire services and consumer magazines, with feature stories and public service advertisements.

National Library Week works. It's a tool for getting librarians together to make the most of limited promotion resources. Success depends on how realistically and enthusiastically the "tool" is put to work. There have been many misconceptions. NLW is not a total library communications or marketing program, but it's not a total waste of time either. Even after twenty-eight years, many review committees, innumerable articles and letters to the editor, National Library Week is a topic for question and comment in the library community. Here are some of the most frequent and favorite questions we receive, and ALA's very biased answers.

"We're tired of National Library Week. Do we have to do it again this year? There's no enthusiasm here. . . ."

If you and your staff are "burned out" by National Library Week, skip it for a year or two. Write a pro-library letter to the editor or try to place a single feature story rather than stage a seven-day extravaganza. NLW should be used only for what it can add to your total communications program. Even if you don't participate, you'll receive positive fallout from national activities, like wire-service stories, a Gene Shalit tribute to libraries on the *Today Show*, etc.

On the other hand, don't forget that National Library Week isn't designed to amuse librarians. You may be tired of it but still make it work to increase public interest. The Morton people probably are really bored with "When it rains it pours," but the public knows their name and buys their salt. Should they write a new slogan because the creative exercise is fun? Do librarians sometimes communicate better with librarians than the rest of the world? Do we sometimes think, discuss, and debate instead of doing?

"Why focus on just one week? Library promotion should happen all year long."

Agreed. NLW should be just one event in a year-round plan for public relations. But there is strength in a special celebration. On the national level, NLW helps ALA receive a listing in the Ad Council's Public Service Advertising Bulletin, a useful endorsement that encourages the media to contribute public service space and time for library messages. National Library Week ads actually are run all year long. In fact, few, if any, of the promotional materials from ALA have specific dates.

NLW is also a good occasion to ask the president for a proclamation about libraries and for librarians and trustees to visit their legislators. Libraries and the ALA don't often get news coverage. NLW generates attention. At the local level it's a great time to have a party and to remind the public that the library is alive, well, and ready to serve.

The following news report from the June 8, 1981, LJ/SLJ *Hotline* demonstrates very well how the week can be put to good use:

> Barbara Allen, director of the Billerica Public Library in Massachusetts, reports on that library's heroic efforts to keep from going down the fiscal drain after Proposition 2½, a measure that severely limits the raising of tax money in towns and cities of Massachusetts. Faced with possible disaster, the library, just a year in its new building, chose National Library Week for a "big birthday bash" that made the library and its many activities highly visible. It also gave the opportunity to make very public the great increase in library activity drawn by the town's new library: circulation up 20 percent, reference questions and registrations each up 60 percent and a new and active Friends organization. The upshot: while schools, recreation, and even fire and police services took cuts, the library came through the annual budget process with essentially the same budget as last year's. When HOTLINE spoke to Ms. Allen, she said that they had won the approval for their budget from the Finance Commission, and expected no trouble in going all the way through the town meeting. The Billerica Public Library will not—as had been feared— have to cut services and lay off staff.

"Why are all your posters for public libraries? For kids? For adults? Too complicated? Too simple?"

Believe it or not, we hear many conflicting complaints about the graphics. One librarian may think a poster is too sophisticated, and another will say it's too juvenile. We know that we'll never have a poster or slogan that will suit everyone. *Chacun a son gout*! But again, let's keep in mind that the message should speak to the library's public, not just the library's staff. You may be repelled personally by Miss Piggy, but she might be a most divine attention-getting spokespig for your library.

The emphasis on public libraries is another matter. NLW can and should work for all types of libraries. ALA's national campaign has given most attention to public libraries because they're the most visible. But we are working hard to enlarge the focus of our publicity efforts and are constantly on the watch for interesting research, news, and feature ideas from school, academic, and special libraries. All suggestions are welcome.

The graphics budget does not make it possible to produce special posters and promotional materials for every type of library. And NLW slogans and graphics have to work for all, from the largest research library to the smallest bookmobile. A big job, but we think it's healthy exercise. The library world has freely fragmented itself. But don't we really have much in common? And don't people think of *their* library, be it school, public or whatever, when they see or hear a library pitch? The ALA materials should be just the starting place for your promotions. We urge you to adapt the slogans and graphics, radio and TV materials. Make them work well for your library, or media center, or information center.

"Why isn't there one national theme for National Library Week? We bought ALA posters and then found out that everybody else in our county had declared a different theme than the one you announced."

Upstart, a commercial firm, produces National Library Week materials and declares it own theme. Several state library associations produce National Library Week materials and declare their own themes. While ALA's theme and graphics are "official," they're not the only choice, and it's a free country. We think there's much to be gained by working together with a single national theme. We'd much rather have librarians celebrate National Library Week with the materials they judge the best, than have them do nothing until they're inspired by the ALA graphics. (We also never miss a chance to remind our colleagues that any income ALA generates through the sale of NLW materials is reinvested in the year-round public service advertising campaign for libraries.)

"Who cares about yet another week? National Library Week is about as relevant as national pickle week!"

What's so irrelevant about pickles? Do we take ourselves too seriously? National Library Week isn't a solemn observance or weighty occasion. It has a lighthearted spirit that does not detract from the importance of libraries. We've already talked about how a special "week" can generate special attention. In the case of libraries, it can help to humanize an institution that may seem forbidding. NLW is a chance to take a breath, congratulate ourselves, thank our staff, and let our public know us a little better.

"We always get things too late. Why don't you announce the theme earlier and start sending our materials earlier so we can have some time to plan?"

This is the best question of all, and the one that makes us groan and promise to do better. In our never-ending search for the perfect NLW campaign, and with the crush of orders and activities that have tripled the frenzy in ALA's Public Information Office, we have been chronically late in completing NLW plans. This must change. The 1983 campaign was previewed at ALA's Annual Conference, July 1982. Materials were ready for distribution in the fall of 1982. We've had to struggle to get on this schedule and make it a part of the National Library Week tradition.

Any further questions? We hope so. We want them. We want the complaints too. The promotion tool, National Library Week, has to make sense to local libraries. We need to keep in touch. We need your ideas for the annual publicity book. National Library Week needs you, and we hope you'll agree that you need National Library Week.

Louise Condak Liebold

What Makes a John Cotton Dana Award Winner?

Active promotion of public libraries was one of the greatest and most novel contributions of John Cotton Dana (1856–1929) to the practice of librarianship. Beginning with his first position as librarian at the Denver Public Library, Dana devoted much energy to informing newspaper editors about the plans of the then-new library, to publishing bulletins about it, and to inviting educational and civic leaders to give public lectures there. He persisted in his enthusiastic promotion throughout his career, even though it was generally frowned upon by the library profession, especially at the beginning. Dana's many other innovations included establishment of the first children's room in the United States and the first branch library devoted to the business community. In 1946, the H. W. Wilson Company and the American Library Association began an annual award in Dana's honor to be presented to outstanding library public relations programs, the John Cotton Dana Library Public Relations Award (JCD).

SOME OTHER FACTS

The award today is cosponsored by the Public Relations Section of ALA's Library Administration and Management Association (LAMA) and the H. W. Wilson Company. The H. W. Wilson Company acts as host at both the judging session in New York and the Annual Conference Reception. In the very early days, the number attending the reception was as small as 20. Today, that number has topped 500! The judges for the JCD Committee are personal members of the Public Relations Section of LAMA, selected by the chair-elect each spring for the coming year. They are people with a special interest in and extensive knowledge of

P.R. programs, and with excellent taste. They are chosen from a variety of geographical areas, types of libraries, and levels of library employment. They usually are ten in number and they serve terms of two years; their terms are staggered, so that at no time is there an entire panel of new judges.

HOW TO ENTER THE JCD AWARD COMPETITION

The H. W. Wilson Company publishes an annual *John Cotton Dana Library Public Relations Award Contest* brochure. Read it carefully because the rules and regulations have to be followed. They are determined by the John Cotton Dana Committee and change slightly from year to year.

THE ENTRY

Methods of presentation will vary from library to library. Programs featuring film, video, or music are all useful to a large library in establishing a vital communication with patrons and potential library users. A small library may accomplish the same results through ads in the local newspaper or a poster campaign.[1] Entries may be entered in either scrapbook or audiovisual format. Most libraries submit a scrapbook.

You don't have to create or make your own scrapbook. Go to the local stationery store and buy a sturdy scrapbook, one no larger than 12″ × 15″. Larger entries will *not be considered* and will be eliminated immediately. Do not use rings for binding. Be sure the scrapbook is well bound before you buy it and after you have completed it. Too many entries arrive for judging in poor and unjudgable condition.

Here are the suggestions of former JCD judges on how to be a winner:

DO

Do read the *JOHN COTTON DANA LIBRARY PUBLIC RELATIONS AWARDS* contest brochure (published by the H. W. Wilson Company) very carefully!!! For a copy, contact: Executive Secretary, LAMA, American Library Association, 50 E. Huron St., Chicago, Ill. 60611.

Do keep the scrapbook down to specified size . . . no larger than 12″ × 15″.

Do remember to fill out the *Fact Sheet* supplied. It is *very important* information for the judges. Include an extra narrative with your scrapbook if it is necessary.

Do watch your grammar and spelling. The contest is *not* an English test, but how you use your words does affect your public image.

Do remember to keep submitted materials within time span allowed in rules and regulations. Some people include items that are four years old!

Do borrow some winning entries (scrapbooks and audiovisual materials) from ALA Headquarters Library, 50 E. Huron St., Chicago, Ill. 60611. Winning entries are on loan to ALA for two years and then they are returned to their owners.

Do give yourself plenty of time to prepare your entry . . . time "to jell" and time to work at it. Have others proofread it . . . and *lots of luck!*

DON'T

Don't submit several entries . . . "only one to a customer."

Don't make it a photo album. Some photos, yes, but not an entire scrapbook.

Don't use heavy cardboard or wood for pages (or cover) in scrapbook. They don't hold up and they certainly weigh the book and the judges down!

Don't try hand-lettering in a scrapbook unless someone on staff is a calligrapher. Use a good typewriter or Instantype for your headlines, etc.

Don't use copyrighted cartoon characters (Snoopy, etc.) in your flyers.

Don't decorate the scrapbook with all kinds of dingbats and doo-dads that have *nothing* to do with the contents of the scrapbook.

Don't submit the cost of the scrapbook in your *Fact Sheet.* What the judges are looking for is the cost of the public relations program or project your entry is about.

Don't pad the scrapbook with superfluous items.

Don't submit volumes and volumes of materials. Keep it down to one, at most, two scrapbooks. *Quality, not quantity,* should be stressed.

Don't send individual items (brochures, newsletters, etc.). For an entry to be considered, it *must be* a scrapbook or A-V entry.

Don't put every single piece of correspondence in your scrapbook. Be selective.

Don't prepare a special introductory TV tape spot just for the JCD judges. It's not necessary.

THE AWARDS

Two kinds of awards are given. The top award, which we call the John Cotton Dana, is given to a few. It is a general award and it honors comprehensive annual public relations programs. The next one, the special award, is given to special public relations projects. You should be proud to win either one!

It's a long hard week for the judges. Their day begins at 8 A.M. when they are picked up by a van and taken to the H. W. Wilson Company in the Bronx, where they spend one week together in one large room, with time off for coffee breaks, lunch (in the building), and other necessities. It's a week of work. Each day ends at about 4:30 P.M. When they are first faced with hundreds of entries on Day One, they wonder if they'll be able to finish it all. They do. There's laughter, and arguments, and on the last day, when the final decisions must be reviewed and the citations written, there are some very healthy disagreements. It sometimes sounds like a courtroom. Most votes are unanimous at this point, but many times the voting is split. It's rough. So, voices do rise on Friday morning of the last day of judging, but they are caring voices. The judges all go home as they came, friends.

IF YOU LOSE

If you thought you really should have been a winner and want to know why you didn't win, you can find out. The judges are fair and their decision is final. Why, you might have even made it all the way to the finals on Friday morning. The letter from the JCD chairperson will tell you if your entry did make it that far. So, you still want to know, "why not me?" Drop a line to the current John Cotton Dana Committee chairperson and ask your question. He or she will look over the evaluation sheets made out by the judges and write you a letter with as many of the judges' comments as he or she feels will be helpful to you.

You might want to become a JCD judge yourself. Get involved in the Public Relations Section. It's a good experience and you meet others who, like yourself, are interested in improving public relations in libraries. You learn and you share with others.

Note

1. "Put Your Library on the Map." 1983 John Cotton Dana entry form. New York: Wilson, 1983.

Margaret Chartrand

Running a Conference Swap 'n' Shop

The informal communication of ideas has always been one of the main benefits of attending conferences. But the Library Administration and Management Association (LAMA) Public Relations Section has taken this informal communication of ideas to a new height with its "swap 'n' shop" sessions in library public relations.

The concept is fairly simple and can work for any size conference. What follows is an organizational road map.

The idea is to set up a situation where a conference goer can gather solutions to P.R. problems either by finding examples of the solution among a quantity of published materials or by consulting a P.R. expert about a particular problem.

Here's how it works. You are the organizer.

1. Get yourself on the conference program for at least a three-hour time slot. Try and find a location that is central to the conference and preferably close to the exhibit area. What you are attempting to do is to provide the conference goer with an easy opportunity to blast through quickly or browse, whatever the schedule permits.

2. You must line up an individual and address to which the swap 'n' shop material can be mailed in advance and collected. You would be well advised to obtain a commitment from this "angel" to have the material moved to the swap 'n' shop conference location on the day of the event.

3. Now that you have the address for mailing you must notify the libraries (usually their P.R. offices) that you would be grateful to receive their best efforts in library promotional material. State the number of copies of each you would like to make

available. For the ALA annual conference we ask for 300 copies of each item to be mailed. You will also send this information to the library journals and newsletters. You want to give the libraries plenty of time so that these large packages can be posted "library rate" and arrive on time. This is the material conference goers can pick up and take away with them.

4. The real fun begins now. You must decide what areas you want your experts to address. You might decide on such areas as how to write news releases; how to get public service announcements on radio and television; how to do audiovisual presentations—slide shows, videotapes, radio and television commercials, films; how to promote bond issues; how to produce an annual report, flyer, brochure or poster; how to program for adults, young adults, children; how to run library orientation; how to run special events; how to do effective exhibits; how to form Friends groups and what to do when they are formed; how to plan a P.R. program and budget for it; how to reach out to your community; how to build support with the politicians; or how to do anything else that might help your library build support, attract users, or make the community better aware of your services.

5. You have the topics. Now you must find the P.R. experts, not an easy task. Choose two or three libraries whose material you know and admire. Call their P.R. people and chat. Each conversation will yield more contacts to be approached and, before long, you will have your network. Write to them formally inviting their participation, assigning them a topic, and telling them what kind of situation they can expect to find. Ask them to arrive at a specific time on swap 'n' shop day to help open boxes and set up the tables. Note: this activity is good exercise too.

Expect a few experts to cancel out and be prepared to call on your friends in this event to fill in at the last minute. Any full-time library P.R. person will be able to talk knowledgeably about the topics mentioned. The trouble will really begin if you divide the topics by type of library—public, school, university, multitype, special, military—the how-to-do-it is the same information but the audience and its level of sophistication are different.

One more word of advice. Try to choose enthusiastic, outgoing experts who love to approach strangers and who can be persuaded to provide their own backup material to their topic. More on this later.

6. The content of the program is set up. Now is the time to turn your attention to promoting your program. Meet the deadline for the conference program. Prepare a news release and send it to some or all of the following places: ALA Public Information Office, state library association newsletters, library schools, library journals including ALA division newsletters, national and/or local media, any mailing list of libraries to which you might have access. You will already have made up your mailing list when you sent out the call for library promotional material. And don't forget to send it to participants and other individuals you have contacted.

7. By this time you should be thinking about setting up the room for the big day. Depending on the conference arrangements, you may have had to make furniture requests very far in advance. In any case here are some of the items you will have to think about.

Signs and signholders for the tables
Tables; two for each shopping topic and one for each expert
Table coverings
Chairs for the experts
A few water stations with chairs for the shoppers
A microphone for announcements
Easels and appropriate signs for doorways to swap 'n' shop programs
Audiovisual equipment as requested by the experts
Flyers listing the program topics and experts. (These can also serve as program guides in the conference registration area and as promotion pieces.)
"Gofers" assigned to the experts
Name tags for the experts
"First-aid" box containing scissors, knives, scotch tape, masking tape, pins, tacks, stapler, ruler, pens, pencils, paper pads, paper clips, elastic bands, Magic Markers, chalk, etc.

As you are concentrating now on the physical arrangements you may as well write to five or six library book bag suppliers and ask for 500 samples from each to use at your swap 'n' shop. The shoppers will appreciate it.

8. Backup material for the experts should be provided by the expert. This could take the form of samples of the expert's own work, an audiovisual presentation, a table-top exhibit on the

topic, and/or a one-page handout outlining how-to-do-it. It all helps introduce the expert and the topic for the shopper. You will have to ask your experts what they intend to use so that you can make the physical accommodations. You will also need your experts to help you set up the shopping tables so be sure to give them a time to report for setup (it usually takes two hours for a large swap 'n' shop) and ask them to bring a pair of scissors or knife for the task. Setup time is a good get-acquainted time and a presession coffee will promote goodwill and energy.

9. There are several other activities that can complement a swap 'n' shop program. If there is a library P.R. competition (such as the John Cotton Dana Awards or the Library Public Relations Council Awards), the winning scrapbooks and/or the winning P.R. people can be on hand at swap 'n' shop. They might even mount their audiovisual winning entries in a corner of a large room or in a room adjacent to the swap 'n' shop. You could invite the editors of library public relations publications to set up a table passing out samples and advice. You could invite representatives of library P.R. organizations to set up a table. You could invite publishers of library public relations books to make some available for sale. You could set up an off-the-street critique session where a conference goer could bring in his or her own material for criticism. Naturally if you have any of these additional activities you will mention them in you swap 'n' shop program promotion.

10. Arrive early at the program site. Breathe easily. It's gonna go! Get set up. Greet your participants and shoppers. Watch it all go well. Accept the congratulations for a job well done. Distribute your evaluation sheets with your return address on them. Close the doors. Celebrate and get a good night's sleep.

Kathleen Kelly Rummel

Planning a P.R. Workshop

As library employees, we've been trained to gather, organize, and retrieve information. Woefully lacking, however, has been our training in communications skills . . . techniques in successfully communicating to our users and nonusers that we have the means to make them "information-rich"!

One way to help ourselves, other library employees, board members, and volunteers to develop communications skills and thus become more responsive to our communities, is to increase the availability of our training opportunities, especially those meant to teach interpersonal communication skills, effective library publicity, and P.R. technique (all discussed together in this article under the umbrella of "P.R. workshops"). No library school covers these subjects adequately and few of us are likely to pick up these skills very quickly or easily as we pursue our usual work routines.

Letting users know the outer limits of what library services can mean for them and introducing nonusers to the information and recreation available at the library is, after all, the essence of good library service. If your library has been considering communications, public relations, and publicity workshops, push for them. Annual training opportunities of this type can only result in making you and your library more important to your community.

Putting together any workshop involves four separate phases: (1) developing a clear understanding of what a workshop is and how its planning should be approached; (2) planning the workshop; (3) presenting the workshop; and (4) conducting follow-up and evaluation activities.

WHAT IS A WORKSHOP, ANYWAY?

A workshop is a meeting where people come together for the purpose of *actively* acquiring new information or a new skill. A good workshop will not only spotlight new information, but will motivate and inspire action. It will promote meaningful discussion, encourage better communication, support good group interaction, and develop leadership. The very word *workshop*, tells us that this type of training experience depends upon the active involvement of all who attend.

A good P.R. workshop should do all of these things and should be approached as an audience-involved training experience. A typical workshop might be planned to present an introduction to the basic elements of and resources needed to support "do-it-yourself" library publicity. Or, your workshop might be dedicated to covering only one subject, such as "How to plan, write, and produce library brochures"; "How to produce a slide show"; "How to *listen* more effectively"; "How to put together great displays"; "How to write a radio spot"; or, "Library fundraising techniques." The possibilities are limited only by your audience's interests and needs.

However, regardless of the subject chosen, it is most important to remember to plan your workshop so that it *involves* your audience. "Hands-on" do-it-yourself sessions, group discussions, demonstrations, use of audiovisual and collateral materials, role playing and other techniques, added to the usual lecture format—where appropriate to your topic—will result in a heightened learning experience for everyone involved. And they will help your audience leave the workshop with a better understanding of the topic and the increased confidence needed to actually put their new ideas and skills to work.

NOW THAT I KNOW WHAT IT IS, HOW DO I PLAN ONE?

The first step in planning the P.R. workshop is to establish a planning committee. Members of this group should be sought from among the audience you expect to attend the workshop, to insure reliable and constructive input to the planning process.

The job of the planning committee is to meet as often as necessary to:

Identify and contact resource people to help plan the workshop.
Very specifically identify and define the workshop audience and its training needs.

Select the workshop subject that best fits the audience and
answers its needs.

Establish learning objectives.

Select the topics to be covered at the workshop.

Plan each topic session and discuss techniques to be used in
presenting the topics.

Plan for equipment and materials to be used.

Identify and contact speakers and personnel needed to conduct the workshop.

Prepare a budget and assign tasks.

This list should not seem overwhelming. Your committee may
need to include only two people to plan a small, effective in-
house workshop, or it might include a much larger group planning a year-long series of P.R. workshops for a state-wide audience. In any case, following these planning considerations can
help make your job easier and the end result a better experience
for everyone involved. Here are some details.

Resource People

It is important at the outset of planning to consider what resource people your committee will need to assist in its planning.
There are two ways to approach the selection of resource people: (1) workshop consultant/presenters and (2) advisory resource people.

If the committee has already spent some time identifying its
audience and its training needs, has selected a definite subject,
and has sufficient funds, then consideration should be given to
hiring a workshop consultant/presenter. Many library P.R. consultants and other consultant groups are in the business of
planning and presenting workshops. For one workshop fee, they
will plan content, prepare handout materials, and present the
workshop. During the planning stage, the consultant should be
expected to communicate frequently with the planning committee and to submit a workshop plan to the committee for
approval well in advance of the workshop itself.

The committee should be prepared to pay for the printing of
handouts; travel, hotel, and meal expenses for the consultant
while at the workshop; rental of all necessary audiovisual
equipment; and the purchase of training materials (glue, pencils, paper, etc.). In addition, the committee can expect a consultant's fee for actually planning and presenting the workshop to

run anywhere from $100 to $500 per workshop day, depending upon the subject and complexity of the workshop; the expertise of the consultant; the size of the audience; and the demands of the planning committee. Keep in mind that this fee covers many days of preparation before the workshop itself.

For consultant recommendations, check with your system, state library, or library association, or ALA's Library Administration and Management Association. LAMA's Public Relations Section has published a list of library P.R. speakers, specialists, and consultants, with information about their expertise and consultant activities. Write to the LAMA office at ALA headquarters for a copy.

As an alternative to hiring a consultant, the committee should consider inviting advisory resource people to its meetings. These people might include subject specialists (area artists, media people, continuing education trainers, etc.), state library or system personnel. They should be experienced in the workshop subject and can be expected to provide valuable ideas on developing the workshop content, format, and structure.

The Audience

The committee's first task is to discuss the workshop audience. Who should attend the workshop? Why? What are the concerns of your potential audience regarding library public relations? What do they *want* to learn? What do they *need* to learn? Is this workshop part of a series? Should it be?

Conducting a survey of your audience's P.R. interests and learning needs is an excellent way to gather information that would be helpful in planning the workshop content. Remember that your audience can include many groups: board members, library staff and administrators, Friend's organizations and volunteers are examples.

Workshop Theme and Learning Objectives

Now you're ready to choose the workshop subject that best fits your audience and its concern. Discuss potential subjects and choose one. Based on the subject chosen, what are your workshop learning objectives? Some might include developing new P.R. skills; motivating the audience to organize and use existing communication skills better; and promoting idea exchanges.

Your learning objectives are the main ingredient of your workshop because they will dictate the rest of your planning:

What topics should be covered to achieve your objectives?

What techniques would best be used in presenting the topics: speeches, discussion groups, small group work, demonstrations, panels, or clinics?

What equipment and materials will be needed? Films, slides, projectors, handouts, etc.?

In choosing techniques, equipment, and materials to be used, consider the size and nature of your audience, the size of your room, arrangements for equipment, seating arrangements, the length of your workshop, and special logistics problems.

Speakers and Personnel

Next, choose your workshop personnel. List the talent or knowledge needed for each workshop session and list the speaker or person you think can best handle it. Depending upon the techniques to be used, you may need more than one person per session, or one person may be able to conduct the entire workshop.

When choosing your speakers, look for those who know how to be invigorating and specific about their topics, and who can understand and relate to your audience and its needs. The more ideas and detailed information your speaker can provide in an entertaining fashion, the better.

Budget and Task Assignments

Your workshop may cost very little to produce. On the other hand, you may need to consider methods of funding. Prepare your budget to include items like speaker's expenses and fees, printing and equipment costs, and other items particular to your needs. Pursue sources for workshop funds: grants, state agency or system support, association funding, individual registration fees, and library board donations are a few possibilities.

To ensure that your planning is completed, committee members should be assigned specific tasks. These tasks will be determined by the content and format you've planned for your workshop.

PRESENTING AND EVALUATING THE WORKSHOP

Plan a quick meeting before the workshop to review final details and to check with the speakers. Be sure people are assigned to handle registration, handouts, and equipment checks. And most of all, be ready to improvise in case of emergency: your speaker doesn't show, your equipment won't work, etc. It happens occasionally to all of us and the most important thing is not to panic. Maintain your sense of humor!

Follow-up and evaluation activities are just as important as prior planning. Prepare a follow-up checklist to remind yourself to do thank-you notes, a final file report, bill payment, and final publicity. Two groups should evaluate the workshop—your audience and the planning committee.

Ask your audience to complete a brief evaluation form at the end of the workshop. Ask for their overall rating of the workshop in terms of its usefulness to them, what parts were most useful and which speakers most effective, what improvements could be made, and what topics they would like to see explored in future workshops. Also, you'll want to ask your planning committee how they felt the workshop did, what could have been done better, what went wrong, and how the next one could be better.

STRETCHING

The best of all P.R. workshops are those that impart a sense of confidence and excitement to members of the audience—*confidence* in their newly developed public relations, publicity, and communications skills, and *excitement* about the new ideas and plans they can put into action for their libraries.

So, when planning a P.R. workshop, *stretch* your imagination! Look for innovative ways to teach and motivate your audience. Neither overestimate nor underestimate what they need to learn about library public relations.

My experience in working with workshop audiences across the country has proven to me that the most appreciated P.R. workshops are those that are the most basic, the most practical, and the most skill-building. The library world runs rampant with librarians who are latent artists, designers, media wizards, publicists, community organizers, fund-raisers, promoters, photographers, and programming geniuses. All they need is someone to help them recognize and develop their own talents. You can be that "someone." Begin today to start planning a P.R. workshop. Whether yours is a public, school, academic, or private library, the new skills you'll help develop will show results in a more involved staff, a more visible library, and a more satisfied public.

A Select Bibliography

PUBLIC RELATIONS

Ayer Public Relations/Publicity Stylebook. Philadelphia: Ayer Pr., 1977.

Black, Sam, ed. *Public Relations in the 1980's.* New York: Pergamon Pr., 1980.

Bloomenthal, H. *Promoting Your Cause.* New York: Funk & Wagnalls, 1971.

Center, Allen H., and Frank Walsh. *Public Relations Practices: Case Studies.* 2nd ed. Englewood Cliffs, N.J.: Prentice-Hall, 1981.

Cutlip, Scott, and Allen Center. *Effective Public Relations.* 5th ed. Englewood Cliffs, N.J.: Prentice-Hall, 1982.

Darrow, Richard, ed. *Dartnell Public Relations Handbook.* Chicago: Dartnell, 1968.

Golden, H. *How to Plan/Produce/Publicize Special Events.* New York: Oceana, 1960.

Jacobs, H. *Practical Publicity.* New York: McGraw-Hill, 1964.

Klein, T., and F. Danzig. *How to Be Heard: Making the Media Work for You.* New York: Macmillan, 1974.

Kotler, Philip. *Marketing for Nonprofit Organizations.* 2nd ed. Englewood Cliffs, N.J.: Prentice-Hall, 1982.

Lesly, Philip. *Lesly's Public Relations Handbook.* Englewood Cliffs, N.J.: Prentice-Hall, 1983.

Nolte, Lawrence W. *Fundamentals of Public Relations.* New York: Pergamon Pr., 1979.

Norton, Alice. *Public Relations: Information Sources.* Detroit: Gale, 1970.

Oaks, R. *Communications by Objective: How Non-Profit Organizations Can Build Better Internal Public Relations.* S. Plainfield, N.J.: Groupwork, 1977.

O'Brien, R. *Publicity: How to Get It.* New York: Harper & Row, 1977.

Public Relations Guides for Nonprofit Organizations. 6 booklets. New York: Public Relations Society of America, 1977.

Ross, Robert D. *The Management of Public Relations.* New York: Wiley, 1977.

Seitel, Fraser P. *The Practice of Public Relations.* Columbus, Ohio: Merrill, 1980.

Simon, Raymond. *Publicity and Public Relations Worktext.* Columbus, Ohio: Grid, 1983.

Stephenson, Howard. *Handbook of Public Relations.* 2nd ed. New York: McGraw-Hill, 1971.

Wagner, G. *Publicity Forum.* New York: Weiner, 1977.

Weiner, Richard. *Professional's Guide to Publicity.* 2nd ed. New York: Weiner, 1979.

GENERAL LIBRARY PUBLIC RELATIONS

Angoff, A., ed. *Public Relations for Libraries: Essays in Communications Techniques.* Westport, Conn.: Greenwood Pr., 1973.

Baeckler, V. *PR for Pennies: Low Cost Library Public Relations.* Hopewell, N.J.: Sources, 1978.

———. *Sparkle! PR for Library Staff.* Hopewell, N.J.: Sources, 1980.

———, and L. Larson. *Go, Pep and Pop: 250 Tested Ideas for Lively Libraries.* New York: Unabashed Librarian, 1976.

Barber, Peggy, ed. *68 Great Ideas: The Library Awareness Handbook.* Chicago: American Library Assn., 1982.

Barrow, P. "Public Relations Starts at Home." *Ontario Library Review* 59:196–97 (September, 1975).

"Be Aggressive!" *Unabashed Librarian* 29:9 (1978).

Berry, J. N. "Marketization of Libraries." *Library Journal* 106:5 (January 1, 1981).

———. "Test of the Marketplace." *Library Journal* 104:1605 (September 1, 1979).

Boaz, Martha. "Library Public Relations and Publicity for Survival." *California Librarian* 38:35–39 (October, 1977).

Cabeceiras, James. *The Multimedia Library: Materials Selection and Use.* 2nd ed. New York: Academic Pr., 1982.

Chase's Calendar of Annual Events. Flint, Mich.: Apple Tree Pr., 1958– . Annual.

Cummins, T. R. "Displays." *Unabashed Librarian* 36:1 (1980).

Darling, M. J. "Public Relations Inservice Training." *Unabashed Librarian* 12:15–16 (Summer, 1974).

DeHart, Florence. *The Librarian's Psychological Commitments: Human Relations in Librarianship.* Westport, Conn.: Greenwood Pr., 1979.

Douglis, Phil. "Develop Yourself in Photography." *Library Imagination Paper* 3:4 (Fall, 1981).

Edsall, Marian. *Harried Librarian's Guide to Public Relations Resources*. Madison, Wis.: Coordinated Library Information Programs, 1976.

———. *Library Promotion Handbook*. Phoenix: Oryx Pr., 1980.

Ehli, G. "Special Report: PR and the Newsletter." *Wilson Library Bulletin* 53: 213–14 (November, 1978).

Fontaine, Sue. "Off the Wall—How to Do Slide Tape Shows." *Library Imagination Paper* 5:4 (Winter, 1983).

———. "P.R. Tick/Click." Chicago: American Library Assn., 1976. (30 min. slide/tape.)

———. *Teaching Public Relations for Small Libraries: A Course Manual*. Des Moines: State Library Commission of Iowa, 1978.

Franklin, L. C. *Library Display Ideas*. Jefferson, N.C.: McFarland, 1980.

Garvey, Mona. *Library Displays: Their Purpose, Construction, and Use*. New York: Wilson, 1969.

———. *Library Public Relations: A Practical Handbook*. New York: Wilson, 1980.

Glaser, Fred. "Public Relations." In *Facilities Funding Finesse*, edited by Richard Hall, pp. 20–24. Chicago: American Library Assn., 1982.

Harrison, K. C. *Public Relations for Librarians*. Lexington, Mass.: Lexington Books, 1982.

Hicks, Warren B., and Alma M. Tillin. *Managing Multimedia Libraries*. New York: Bowker, 1977.

"John Cotton Dana Issue." *LIPP (Library Insights, Promotions, and Programs)*. August issue. Annual.

Kies, Cosette. *Problems in Library Public Relations*. New York: Bowker, 1974.

Kohn, Rita, and Krysta Tepper. *You Can Do It: A PR Skills Manual for Librarians*. Metuchen, N.J.: Scarecrow Pr., 1981.

Latshaw, P. H. "Evaluating Your Public Relations Program." *Ohio Library Association Bulletin* 48:32–34 (April, 1978).

Leerburger, Benedict. *Marketing the Library*. New York: Knowledge Industry Publications, 1982.

Mallery, Mary S., and Ralph E. DeVore. *A Sign System for Libraries*. Chicago: American Library Assn., 1982.

Manley, W. "Facing the Public." *Wilson Library Bulletin* 55:366–67 (January, 1981).

Mathews, Ann J. *Communicate! A Librarian's Guide to Interpersonal Relations*. Chicago: American Library Assn., 1983.

Moran, Irene, ed. *PRepare: The Library Public Relations Recipe Book*. Chicago: Library Administration and Management Assn., 1978.

O'Donnell, P. "Ways in Which Librarians Can Inform the Public About

Services and Resources." *Wyoming Library Roundup* 28:31–38 (June, 1973).

Pollett, Dorothy, and Peter Haskell. *Sign Systems for Libraries.* New York: Bowker, 1979.

Powell, Judith W., and Robert B. LeLieuvre. *Peoplework: Communications Dynamics for Librarians.* Chicago: American Library Assn., 1979.

"Public Awareness: Is Your Library's Image What It Could Be?" Chicago: American Library Assn., 1982. Set of 60-min. cassettes: No. 82/431–School Libraries/Media Centers; no. 82/432–Academic Libraries; no. 82/433–Multi-Type Libraries, Federated Systems and State Agencies; no. 82/434–Public Libraries.

"Public Relations Issue." *Catholic Library World.* (February, 1975 and March, 1979).

Schmidt, J. "Outline for an Online Public Relations Program." *Online Review* 2: 47–50 (October, 1978).

Sherman, Steve. *ABC's of Library Promotion.* 2nd ed. Metuchen, N.J.: Scarecrow Pr., 1980.

Stiles, Florence. "Action, How to Get It Started: Effective Public Relations Techniques." *Iowa Library Quarterly* 21:292–93 (July, 1972).

Usherwood, R. C. "Do You Relate?" *Aslib Proceedings* 33:393–99 (October, 1981).

———. "Library Public Relations: An Introduction." In *Studies in Library Management,* edited by C. Bingley, pp. 114–33. Hamden, Conn.: Shoe String Pr., 1975.

Van Zanten, F. "Fine Receipt Is Good PR." *Unabashed Librarian* 36:3 (1980).

Wedgeworth, Robert, ed. "Public Relations." *ALA Yearbook: A Review of Library Events.* Chicago: American Library Assn., 1976– . Annual.

PUBLIC LIBRARIES

Barron, D. D., and C. C. Curran. "Assessing the Information Needs of Rural People." *Library Trends* 28:619–31 (Spring, 1980).

Bolton, W. T. "Life Style Research; An Aid to Promoting Public Libraries." *Library Journal* 107:963–68 (May 15, 1982).

Brunton, D. W. "Library Newsletter Distributed in Supermarkets." *Unabashed Librarian* 16:31 (Summer, 1975).

Bryan, Carol. "Giving and Getting Good Interviews." *Library Imagination Paper* 4:4 (Spring, 1982).

———. "Puppets . . . They're Only Human." *Library Imagination Paper* 3:4 (Summer, 1981).

Christo, Steve. "Crowd-Getter PR Tips and Ideas for Your Film Program." *Library Imagination Paper* 2:4 (Winter, 1980).

Dance, James C. "Public Relations for the Smaller Library." (Small Libraries Publication Series, no. 4.) Chicago: Library Administration and Management Assn., 1979.

Dolnick, Sandy, ed. *Friends of the Library Sourcebook.* Chicago: American Library Assn., 1980.

Dragon, A. C. "Marketing the Library." *Wilson Library Bulletin* 53:498–502 (March, 1979).

Driscoll, A. "Dilemma for Today's Public Librarians; The Problem Patron." *Southeastern Librarian* 30:15–21 (Spring, 1980).

Edsall, M. S. "Programming with a Purpose." *Show-Me Libraries* 31:38–40 (February, 1980).

Eisner, J. "Why a Communitywide Newsletter?" *Unabashed Librarian* 21:13–14 (1976).

Garvey, Mona. "Display 6-Pack: A Multi-Media Display Packet for Libraries." Atlanta: M. G. Associates, 1974.

———. *Teaching Displays.* Hamden, Conn.: Shoe String Pr., 1972.

———. "Shapes to Shape Up Your Bulletin Board." *Library Imagination Paper* 1:4 (Spring, 1979).

Glazer, Fred. "Promote or Perish." *Arkansas Libraries* 44:12–17 (Spring, 1980).

Glover, P. "Planning Participation and Public Relations: Essentials for Trustees." *Tennessee Librarian* 30:16–18 (Fall, 1978).

Hamilton, L. C. "Public Relations in the Children's Department and Beyond." *Nebraska Library Association Quarterly* 13:30–31 (Spring, 1981).

Hartnett, J. "Public Relations; Putting $$$ Where It Counts." *Connecticut Libraries* 22:27 (Fall, 1979).

Kohn, Rita. "Making Money, Making Friends." *Library Imagination Paper* 4:4 (Winter, 1982).

Lewis, Fran. "Make Your Library a Life in the Day of the Special Patron." *Library Imagination Paper* 2:4 (Summer, 1980).

Liebold, Louise. "Two for the Road." *Library Imagination Paper* 1:4 (Fall, 1979).

Livingston, B. "How to Tap Funding from Private/Public Sources." *Library Journal* 104:2610–11 (December 15, 1979).

McCorran, C. E. "Public Awareness in Rural Libraries." *West Virginia Libraries* 34:8–10 (Summer, 1981).

McNeely, K. "Public Relations in the Library." *Idaho Librarian* 27:10–14 (January, 1975).

Nelson, M. G. "Making Room for an Unfamiliar Cat." *Wilson Library Bulletin* 56:567 (April, 1982).

Norton, Alice. "Public Relations—Its Meaning and Benefits." In *Local*

Public Library Administration, edited by E. Altman, pp. 47–60. 2nd rev. ed. Chicago: American Library Assn., 1980.

———. "Why Does a Public Library Need Public Relations?" *Catholic Library World* 48:289–91 (February, 1977).

Proeschel, Diana C. "Getting Started." *Public Libraries* 17:6–7 (Spring, 1978).

———. ———. (Expanded version.) *Unabashed Librarian* 26:5–8, 1978.

———. "Leaders Are Readers: The Making of an Exhibit." *Library Imagination Paper* 2:4 (Fall, 1980).

Rice, Betty. *Public Relations for Public Libraries: Creative Problem Solving.* New York: Wilson, 1972.

Scilken, Marvin. "Realism in Public Library Public Relations." *Library Journal* 97:1246–47 (April 1, 1972).

Spiegler, G. "Advertise! It Can Work for You." *West Virginia Libraries* 30:42–43 (Fall-Winter, 1977).

Swan, James. "New Visibility for the Small Public Library." *Wilson Library Bulletin* 51:424–29 (January, 1977).

Usherwood, R. C. *The Visible Library: Practical PR for Public Libraries.* Phoenix: Oryx Pr., 1981.

Webber, B. "Strong Public Relations a Key Ingredient in Successful Library Events." *Michigan Librarian* 39:12–13 (Summer, 1973).

Wright, A. "Thirst for Publicity." *New Library World* 79:253–54 (January, 1978).

Young, Virginia. *The Library Trustee: A Practical Guidebook.* 3rd ed. New York: Bowker, 1978.

ACADEMIC LIBRARIES

Alsmeyer, H. L. "Academic Library—Campus Community Communications." *Catholic Library World* 50:336–39 (March, 1979).

Apple, M. "Public Relations in Academic Libraries." *Michigan Librarian* 39:8–9 (Summer, 1973).

Brickman, Sally. "Academic Library Needs; A Planned Communications Program." *Catholic Library World* 54:137–39 (October, 1981).

Dragon, A. C. "Marketing the Library." *Wilson Library Bulletin* 53:498–502 (March, 1979).

Edinger, J. A. "Marketing Library Services." *College and Research Libraries* 41:328–32 (July, 1980).

Gwynn, M. B. "Marketing the Law School Library." *Law Library Journal* 71:234–46 (May, 1978).

Heathcote, D. "Public Relations and Publicity." In *Libraries in Higher Education: The User Approach to Service*, edited by John Cowley. Hamden, Conn.: Linnet Books, 1975.

Mathew, R. M. "Modern Marketing Techniques for the Effective Management of University Libraries." *Herald of Library Science* 19:198–201 (July, 1980).

Miller, L. A. "Liaison Work in the Academic Library." *RQ* 16:213–15 (Spring, 1977).

New, D. E. "Community Analysis for Academic Libraries Workshop." *Unabashed Librarian* 35:11 (1980).

Perry, T. "Selling of Media on Campus." *Florida Media Quarterly* 3:22–24 (Summer-Fall, 1977).

Pollet, D. "New Directions in Library Signage: You Can Get There from Here." *Wilson Library Bulletin* 50:456–62 (February, 1976).

Shires, N. "Campus Information Office: A Valuable Service to Academic Libraries." *North Carolina Libraries* 39:3–7 (Winter, 1981).

Winikoff, E. A. "Phase In: A University Public Relations Campaign." *Ohio Media Spectrum* 29:52–54 (May, 1977).

SCHOOL LIBRARIES

Baeckler, Virginia. "The Library Should Be Seen and Heard." *The Book Report* 1:29 (May/June, 1982).

Barry, A. "School Library Public Relations Program." *Ohio Association School Librarians Bulletin* 27:15 (May, 1975).

Basic School PR Guide. [Arlington], Va.: National School Public Relations Assn., 1980.

Behm, Mary, ed. *Practical Public Relations: Effective PR Techniques for School Library Media Specialists.* Toledo: Ohio Education Library/Media Assn., 1979.

Blank, P. "How Media Specialists Promote Their Services." *Media and Methods* 17:37–38 (January, 1981).

Bryan, Carol. "Basic Thought Starters for Public Awareness." *The Book Report* 1:23 (May/June, 1982).

Building Public Confidence for Your Schools: A Sourcebook of Proven P.R. Practices. Arlington, Va.: National School Public Relations Assn., 1978.

Edmonds, V. "Media and Public Relations." *Ohio Media Spectrum* 29:7–10 (May, 1977).

Edsall, Marion. *Practical PR for School Library Media Centers.* New York: Neal Schuman, 1983.

Eisenberg, M. B. "View from the Other Side." *School Library Journal* 27:39 (December, 1980).

Fredericka, Terri. "The Case for Public Awareness of School Media Programs." *The Book Report* 1:20 (May/June, 1982).

"Good Public Relations." In *Pathfinder: An Operational Guide for the*

School Librarian, edited by Patricia Freeman, pp. 114–33. New York: Harper & Row, 1975.

Green, S. A. "Merchandising Techniques and Libraries." *School Library Journal* 28:35–39 (September, 1981).

Harvard, C., and P. Healey. "Moving Media with a Messenger." *School Library Journal* 28:34 (December, 1981).

Heller, D. H. "Public Relations in School Media Centers: Planning and Performing." *Ohio Media Spectrum* 8:3 (1981).

Henderson, D. C. "School Library and Community Involvement." *Louisiana Library Association Bulletin* 41:48–49 (Winter, 1979).

Kies, Cosette. *Projecting a Positive Image through Public Relations.* (School Media Centers: Focus on Trends and Issues, no. 2) Chicago: American Library Assn./American Assn. of School Librarians, 1979.

Kindred, Leslie, et al. *The School and Community Relations.* 2nd ed. Englewood Cliffs, N.J.: Prentice-Hall, 1976.

Kohn, Rita, and Krysta Tepper. *Have You Got What They Want? Public Relations Strategies for the School Librarian-Media Specialist.* Metuchen, N.J.: Scarecrow Pr., 1982.

Lantz, J. "Public Relations: The Positive Response." *Ohio Media Spectrum* 29:4–6 (May, 1977).

Laughlin, M. "Action Activities: A Program of PR." *Learning Today* 9:90–92 (Summer-Fall, 1976).

McNerney, M. E. "School Librarian and Public Relations: Showing That You Care." *Catholic Library World* 50:334–35 (March, 1979).

Montgomery, Ann. M. "Beyond School Walls: A Misconception about PR." *Ohio Media Spectrum* 34:22–28 (Fall, 1982).

———. "Public Relations in School Media Centers: Planning and Performing. Part II: Performing." *Ohio Media Spectrum* 8:3 (1981).

Perica, Esther. "Blueprint for Community Outreach." *Ohio Media Spectrum* 34:13–16 (Fall, 1982).

Petrone, Cheryl, and Esther Perica. "The Schools and the Teens." *LIPP (Library Insights, Promotion and Programs)* 7:3 (October, 1982).

"Promoting Media Center Services." In *Media Center Management,* edited by W. T. Schmid, pp. 148–55. New York: Hastings House, 1980.

"Public Relations Issue." *Ohio Media Spectrum* 29:4 (May, 1977).

Saks, L. "Public Schools and Public Relations; Needed: A Positve Posture." *Michigan Librarian* 44:13–14 (Spring, 1978).

"School Library PR: A Neglected Angle." *Library PR News* 1–4 (September/October, 1980).

Stith, Linda, and Ed Klee. "School and Public Library Corporation— Another Public Relations Must!" *Ohio Media Spectrum* 34:17–21 (Fall, 1982).

Thomas, R. "Plus Factor; Publicizing Library/Media Utilization and Services." *School Library Journal* 28:35 (May, 1982).

Wiget, Lawrence A. "Successful Public Relations: It Takes More Than Money." *Ohio Media Spectrum* 34:10–12 (Fall, 1982).

OTHER TYPES OF LIBRARIES

Hannaford, C. "Promotion of a Church Library." *Drexel Library Quarterly* 6:134–39 (April, 1970).
"Library Public Relations Issue." *Catholic Library World* 46:272–317 (February, 1975).
Raburn, Josephine. "Public Relations for a Special Public." *Special Libraries* 60:647–50 (December, 1969).
Smith, Ruth S. *Getting the Books off the Shelves: Making the Most of Your Congregation's Library*. New York: Seabury, 1979.
Titley, Joan. "Library and Its Public: Identification and Communications." In *Handbook of Medical Library Practice*, 4th ed., pp. 37–67. Chicago: Medical Library Assn., 1982.

PUBLICATIONS, ORGANIZATIONS, AND OTHER SOURCES

Publications

American Library Association, 50 East Huron Street, Chicago, Illinois 60611. Publishes documents, cassette tapes, etc., many of which aid in public relations. Write to Order Department for a current catalog of publications.
The Get Ready Sheet. Unique semimonthly publication includes media tie-in information, author promotion itineraries, soon-to-be-released movies, etc. Six issues a year, $17.00. Mid-York Library System, 1600 Lincoln Avenue, Utica, New York 13502.
The Library Imagination Paper. Carol Bryan, editor. Contains clip art, tips, full page articles and other promotional information for libraries and librarians. Four issues a year, $14.00. 1000 Byus Drive, Charleston, West Virginia 25311.
Library Insights, Promotion and Programs (LIPP). Dawn Heller and Ann Montgomery, editors. Monthly newsletter with ideas and insights on promotion. $15.00 a year, P.O. Box 431, LaGrange, Illinois 60525.
Library Publicity Clippings. Quarterly publication featuring ready-made radio/television spots. $12.00 a year. P.O. Box 742, Santa Ana, California 92702.
Public Relations Plus. Public Relations Committee. Public Libraries Section of the New York Library Association. *PR +* is sent regularly to members of the Public Libraries Section of NYLA. Out-of-state

readers may order single copies from Community Services, Onondaga County Public Library, 327 Montgomery Street, Syracuse, New York 13202.

Show Forth: Bimonthly Display and Publicity Ideas for All Librarians. Linda Campbell Franklin, editor. Contains a potpourri of ideas, displays, calendar ideas, etc. Bimonthly, $12.00 a year. McFarland and Company, Inc., Box 611, Jefferson, North Carolina 28640.

THE U*N*A*B*A*S*H*E*D LIBRARIAN. Marvin H. Scilken, editor. Four issues per year include ideas on all types of library activities, notably public relations. $20.00 a year. G.P.O. Box 2631, New York, N.Y. 10116.

Organizations

Library Public Relations Council. Members receive an annual assortment of library publications produced during the preceding year. Also sponsors an annual award program. $7.50 a year. 60 East 42nd St., Suite 1242, New York, New York 10017.

Public Relations Section. Library Administration and Management Association, a division of the American Library Association. This section presents programs on a myriad of public relations topics each year at the annual American Library Association conference. Year-round activities focus on publications, surveys, standards, awards programs, workshops, and continuing education. Membership in this section is open to all members of the Library Administration and Management Association of the American Library Association, 50 E. Huron Street, Chicago, Illinois 60611.

Other Public Relations committees in the American Library Association include:

LAMA/PRS Public Relations Services to Libraries Committee

LAMA/PRS Public Relations Services to State Library Agencies and Library Associations Committee

Library Instruction Round Table Public Relations/Membership Committee

Public Library Association Armed Forces Librarians Section Public Relations Committee

Young Adult Services Division Public Relations Committee

Sources

John Cotton Dana Library Public Relations Awards. Under the sponsorship of the H. W. Wilson Company, the John Cotton Dana Judging Committee selects the recipients of the annual John Cotton Dana Award(s). These awards are given to libraries for their comprehensive year-long P.R. programs. Special awards are also given for outstanding achievement in single P.R. projects. Brochures are sent to libraries on the H. W. Wilson mailing list in the spring. Additional copies may be obtained from the H. W. Wilson Company, 950 University Avenue, Bronx, New York 10452. Awards are given at the American Library Association summer conference, after which time winning entries may be borrowed through interlibrary loan from the ALA library.

Library Public Relations Workshop Consultants. Chicago: American Library Association, 1983. A list, including qualifications of well-known library P.R. experts available for workshops, speaking engagements, and free-lance assignments.

National Library Week. Posters, buttons, radio/television materials are available to coincide with the annual theme. Write to the Public Information Office, American Library Association, 50 E. Huron St., Chicago, Illinois 60611 for a catalog.

Upstart Library Promotionals. Library promotional items of all kinds. Catalog is available from Box 889, Hagerstown, Maryland 21740.

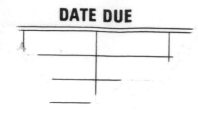